Angela R. Edwards

GOD SAYS

I am Battle-Scar Free:
Testimonies of Abuse Survivors –
Part Seven

Compiled By:
Angela R. Edwards

Foreword By:
Dr. Marilyn E. Porter

Pearly Gates Publishing, LLC, Houston, Texas (USA)

God Says I am Battle-Scar Free:
Testimonies of Abuse Survivors – Part Seven

Copyright © 2021
Angela R. Edwards

All Rights Reserved.
No portion of this publication may be reproduced, stored in an electronic system, or transmitted in any form or by any means (electronic, mechanical, photocopy, recording, or otherwise) without written permission from the publisher. Brief quotations may be used in literary reviews.

Print ISBN 13: 978-1-948853-25-5
Digital ISBN 13: 978-1-948853-26-2
Library of Congress Control Number: 2021936583

Some names and identifying details have been changed to protect the privacy of individuals.

Scripture references are used with permission from Zondervan via Biblegateway.com.
Public Domain.

For information and bulk ordering, contact:
Pearly Gates Publishing, LLC
Angela Edwards, CEO
P.O. Box 62287
Houston, TX 77205
BestSeller@PearlyGatesPublishing.com

Dedication

In loving memory of the countless women, men, and children who have lost their lives at the hands of abusers.

May you always be remembered for the **JOY** you brought to others on this side of Heaven.

Acknowledgments

First and foremost, we give all praise, honor, and glory to **God our Heavenly Father.** Thank You, Lord, for the gift of **LIFE** that You provided each contributor of *God Says I am Battle-Scar Free – Part Seven*. We pray our words give solace to others and that our collective voices guide them to Your Holy Spirit. May our obedience to Your calling effect change in others — both victim and abuser…*one life at a time.*

To each **Contributor** who answered the call to be a part of this project: Many were called, but it was *YOU* who remained. *YOU* chose this time to give voice to your pains from the past. Thank you for your resilience and for sharing intimate details of your life with others. Change begins with each of you. It was not I but **GOD** who chose you for such a time as this. My gratitude extends beyond the skies as we work to save lives through the power of the written word.

To **Marlowe R. Scott**: For many years, you have shared your Battle-Scar Free Staple Poem, *Abuse is NOT love*, with the audience. As it reaches new readers, I pray the words connect with them right where they are in their time of need. I will be forever grateful for your second set of keen eyes on **EVERY** book in the *God Says I am Battle-Scar Free* series. I do not know what I would do without you. Thank you for your parenting, pushing, and prayers throughout my life. I love you to no end and genuinely appreciate everything you do for me.

To **Dr. Marilyn E. Porter**: Well, you showed up and showed out yet again! Your Foreword is just what this project needed as we close out the series. Although I am sad to see it come to an end, I know God has more for both of us on this journey called *"LIFE."* Thank you so much for opening your soul and pouring it out for this seventh time. Your thoughtful words are just what "we" need…**RIGHT NOW.** My prayer for you is that God continues to grace you with higher heights. I love you, Murl!

Last, but **FAR** from least, I believe I can speak for us **ALL** as we thank *GOD* for His whole armor (Ephesians 6:10-18):

The Armor of God

"Finally, be strong in the Lord and in his mighty power. Put on the full armor of God, so that you can take your stand against the devil's schemes. For our struggle is not against flesh and blood, but against the rulers, against the authorities, against the powers of this dark world and against the spiritual forces of evil in the heavenly realms. Therefore, put on the full armor of God, so that when the day of evil comes, you may be able to stand your ground, and after you have done everything, to stand. Stand firm then, with the belt of truth buckled around your waist, with the breastplate of righteousness in place and

with your feet fitted with the readiness that comes from the gospel of peace. In addition to all this, take up the shield of faith, with which you can extinguish all the flaming arrows of the evil one. Take the helmet of salvation and the sword of the Spirit, which is the word of God. And pray in the Spirit on all occasions with all kinds of prayers and requests. With this in mind, be alert and always keep on praying for all the Lord's people."

Father God, we ask that You keep Your loving arms enveloped around victims of abuse in any form as they take back that which was stolen: **FREEDOM** from abuse. In Your Mighty, Matchless Name, we pray.

Amen and Amen.

~ Angela R. Edwards ~

Angela R. Edwards

Foreword

ABUSE takes away our ability to be *FREE*.

ABUSE in any form engages the soul and locks away the processes of the heart where our basic human rights live.

We forget the value of who we are created to be as we assimilate into the:

- Battered and Bruised.
- Teased and Taunted.
- Torched and Terrified.
- Hunted and Haunted.
- Defiled and Dismantled.
- Disrespected and Demanded.
- Starved and Stunned.

In the deepest essence possible, we become nonhuman because our souls are drained of the dignity of **FREEDOM**.

For almost ten years (at the time of this writing), the Battle-Scar Free Movement has given *thousands* of individuals the keys to return to the place of **FREEDOM** in their hearts and souls. The key to that place was simply to tell their stories. Thank you, Angela, for such a bold and brave move that gave a voice to those who had been shamed to silence.

Shame seems like such an unfair place for someone to be—*ESPICIALLY* after their very existence has been violated. Sadly, the human condition permits us to lay shame and guilt on the victim, with the questioning and the need to understand why.

"How could you let them do this to you?" **'they'** ask.

"Why did you stay?" **'they'** question.

"You're such a smart woman/man. It just doesn't make sense!" **'they'** wonder.

Many times, their words (presented in the form of condescending questions) are sincere and well-intended, but they merely create a shame-based noose around the necks of victims. Often, the abuser's words are made to appear to be true!

*"I am the **ONLY** one who loves you!"*

*"**Nobody** will believe you."*

Y'all know those words, whether spoken or heard.

As I sat to pen this final Foreword of the *God Says I Am Battle-Scar Free* book series, my thoughts raced through the many stories that have already been told through the years. I recall a few raw emotions I felt early on from books one and two—when abuse resembled childhood and the convincing of said child that the abuse was 'normal'…that *"This is how everybody lives."* In other past books, many of the abused saw **death** as the only real way out, **BUT GOD!**

MY GOD!

Have we truly become so calloused and cold as a people that we do not hear the muted screams of our friends, family, neighbors, coworkers, church members, grocery clerks, etc.?

Do we still have scales on our eyes and cellophane wrapped around our hearts that block it all out?

There is more than enough information available to educate us on "the signs." The Battle-Scar Free Movement is one of many that shines a bright light on those signs. I believe the truth is that we know. We see. We hear. We sense the fear. And we remain silent because a true and committed abuser uses their power not only to silence their victims but also to silence the community. As a result, **everyone** connected to the trauma is left quieted, afraid, and ashamed — ashamed because they *know*.

WE know…and **WE** do *nothing*.

So, again I say to Angela: Much respect to you, Sis, for pushing past the shame, screaming loudly, and shouting down the barriers that become the stilts and bricks that uphold abuse.

Thank you for allowing yourself to be pushed to the brink of freedom to tell your **own** story.

Thank you for making it a little more difficult for the rage to rule the story.

Thank you for shifting the narrative.

Thank you for becoming the body armor that so many of the survivors needed to break free and tell their stories.

Thank you for turning trauma into triumph.

Thank you for taking the ugly, putrid face of abuse and finding something of value — the ability to become a voice in the darkness for so many. You did that, girl! God bless you for taking the reins and letting your light so shine — and I do mean **SHINE!**

As a woman of faith, power, and intellect, I must confess my own abuse story was one that I was reluctant to share. It was not because I was ashamed, though. Rather, I needed to weigh the benefit for the reader. I asked myself, *"Would it be more advantageous for the reader to only know me as Pastor, Apostle, Leader, and Strong Black Woman* **OR** *would it help the reader to break free of their own chains if they know that I, too — in all my gifting, anointing, strength, and intellect…yes, even I — had known the terror of abuse?"* To God be the glory, it felt best to tell the story! To God be the glory, it felt best to be a part of the healing and the rebuilding of the people!

To the survivors and brave authors of the Battle-Scar Free Movement, I salute and honor you for taking your rightful place in the story: **VICTORY!**

To the God of all creation, thank You for creating this journey for Your children, simply because we **ALL** needed it.

Apostle Dr. Marilyn E. Porter
Founder and Overseer
The Pink Pulpit International Convention of Women in Ministry
www.thepinkpulpit.org

Preface

Approximately ten years ago, from the time of this publication, I publicly shared my abuse survivor story during a conference call with *Motivationally ME* — a platform designed for women to elevate in their God-given assignments, courtesy of Dr. Marilyn E. Porter. At the time, it had been close to 20 years since my story was birthed. I had found myself a victim of domestic violence…a position in which I **never** thought I would be. I have my ex-husband (and my perceived weakness) to "thank" for the experience, for without, I likely would not have realized my strength and the power of my words.

I recall when I first told my story, my grown daughter was on the line. When the time came for the women to provide words of encouragement or simply share their own abbreviated stories, my daughter's voice flowed through with obvious tears behind every word she spoke. It was essential that she heard my truth, as she was approaching treacherous waters in her own life and relationships. In no way did I want her to experience the pain and anguish I endured. Her story is hers to tell, but I will say that she, too, was victimized — and that is enough said. I must add here that my heart was **broken** as I listened to her pour out her heart in what I knew to be a no-judgment zone.

So, here we are…seven books later in the *God Says I am Battle-Scar Free* series. When God initially tasked me to offer the platform to women, men, and teens to tell their horrid tales of survival, I questioned Him: *"Why me, God?"*

His response was one I am sure many others before me heard: *"Because I gave **you** the testimony to tell. You survived. Now, tell it…and uplift others along the way."*

I humbly accepted the assignment and am **OVERJOYED** to say I do not regret one minute of my *"YES!"*

In addition to helping others tell their testimonies (many for the first time), every dollar received has been donated to the Star of Hope Mission in Houston, Texas (USA) in the name of the Battle-Scar Free Movement. The Mission is near and dear to my heart, to the point that I used to volunteer my time as their Domestic Violence Liaison. The women I met were in a place of pain and brokenness. Most were separated from their children and other loved ones. Many others struggled to overcome their source of pain, yet they worked their way through adversity and refused to give up. Just as it has always been from the start, every dollar made from this volume will be given to the

Mission as they continue to help victims from **ALL** walks of life become new.

My prayer is that although this part of my assignment has come to an end with the publication of this book, the numerous stories will continue to resonate and be shared with people worldwide. Healing awaits us **ALL** on the other side of through. Will *YOU* take the journey with me? Grab hold of my hand and the one closest to you, and let us collectively do two things:

1. Show the enemy of our soul (Satan) that he no longer has a right to keep us in bondage; and
2. Give a glory shout of *"HALLELUJAH!"* to **GOD** for His protection throughout our days past and days to come.

Thank you for not finding it robbery to invest your money and your time into reading this beautifully designed piece of literary art. You will not be disappointed.

Angela R. Edwards

Introduction

God is the **Great I AM.** It is **HE** who has been at the helm of the *God Says I am Battle-Scar Free* series since its inception. Before it became a thought, **HE** had already aligned those who would become contributing authors. It was **HE** who wrote the stories before they were experienced.

How can we **NOT** be grateful for what we have gone through?

Now in its seventh and final year of publication, this book has been published to encourage **YOUR** release and **YOUR** renewal. With each new season in your life, there may be times when you feel all alone. From this day forward, know that you are *NEVER* alone. You will read stories within that you can relate to in one way or another. As you flip from page to page, you will likely feel a plethora of negative emotions, including:

- ❖ Rage
- ❖ Sorrow
- ❖ Sympathy
- ❖ Revulsion

You are encouraged to "feel." It is okay. You are human, after all. **Remember: Jesus wept.** Here is the thing, though: By the end of each testimony contained herein, you will stand and applaud each contributor for their boldness and transparency!

This book in **YOUR** hands is no coincidence. Why? Because this is **YOUR** season for a change! If you feel you are wandering through life and have no purpose of living another day, how about letting *SURVIVAL* rise to the top?

On this book's pages, shame, guilt, and horrific accounts of abuse are spotlighted. No longer can they hide and bear down on the *FORMER* victims. Conversely, if your story is like any of what you will read — physical abuse, neglect, fear, abandonment, confusion, failure, or any other traumatic experience — **THIS BOOK IS FOR YOU.**

At the end of this book, resources are provided for you to connect with various organizations for "whatever ails you." They can assist you with being set **FREE**…when you are ready. I pray you are empowered to take that first step…and then another. Reach out for help. Family and friends are ready and waiting for you, even if they are presently unaware that you are under attack by the enemy. Prepare to be surprised at the positive response to your cry for help — especially once you silence the enemy by using the *POWER* of your words.

Remember always:
Abuse comes in **MANY** forms.

The pathway to **FREEDOM** has already been set out before you. Open the door. Walk through it in faith. **GOD** says you are already **BATTLE-SCAR FREE!**

Table of Contents

DEDICATION	VI
ACKNOWLEDGMENTS	VII
FOREWORD	X
PREFACE	XV
INTRODUCTION	XVIII
THE BATTLE-SCAR FREE STAPLE POEM	1
WESLEY HUBBARD	3
From Death to Life	
TONDRA "POETIC SENSE" MOSLEY	9
Champion	
SHGLENDA GREEN	13
Chasing False Love to Finding Unconditional Love	
NIKKI DENISE	23
From 13 to 30-Something, I am Battle-Scar Free	
NAKIA ALLEN	32
Free from Pleasing People	
LAURIE BENOIT	39
This Was the Story of a Broken Girl	
CRAIG MOSLEY, SR.	54
Why Me?	
ALEXANDRA ESPERANCE	59
Black Heart – A Poem	
TOSHA R. DEARBONE	61
Rejection Could Have Killed Me	
TANYA HOLLAND	72
The Narcissist	

REYNA HARRIS-GOYNES 85

    FREE FROM TOXICITY

ALEXANDRA ESPERANCE 91

    SELFISH – A POEM

NIKKI CHEREE 93

    BREATHING AFTER BETRAYAL

MARLOWE SCOTT 105

    THE ABUSIVE TONGUE: WORDS MATTER

LAURA MOSELEY 117

    MY STORY OF PAIN AND PROMISE

ALEXANDRA ESPERANCE 130

    BETRAYAL – A POEM

GOD SAYS I AM BATTLE-SCAR FREE – PART SEVEN CONCLUSION ... 132

MY PLAN TO BREAK THE CYCLE OF ABUSE IN MY LIFE 136

NATIONAL DOMESTIC ABUSE RESOURCES 139

CONNECT WITH PEARLY GATES PUBLISHING 143

THE FACES OF THE FREE 144

God Says I am Battle-Scar Free – Part Seven

The Battle-Scar Free Staple Poem

ABUSE IS NOT LOVE
© 2015 Marlowe R. Scott

Abuse comes in many forms.
In some cultures and homes,
Abuse is the norm.
It's directed at children and adults, too;
Has abuse ever happened to you?
Have scars—seen and unseen—
Impacted this earthly life?
Have loved ones inflicted pains, causing deep strife?
What to do? Where to turn for relief?
There has to be a way to make it through another day.
Help me, Dear Lord; Help me, I pray.
I have heard about Jesus
And how He came to save us.
Is Jesus the answer for me?
If so, this is my plea:
Help me, Dear Jesus.
Help me right now.
At Your throne, I throw my cares and humbly bow.
Please relieve the pain; make it go away.
I believe You can, and this I pray.
Thank You for the warm comfort I now feel.
Thank You, Dear Jesus, because I know You can heal.
Take my abuser under Your care,
So that no one else will feel the pains I bear.

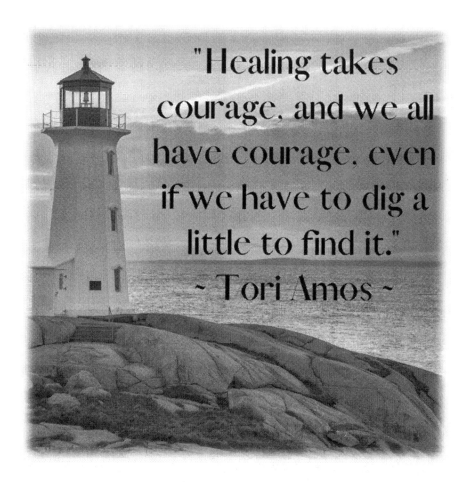

Wesley Hubbard
From Death to Life

Well, what can I say? I did everything in the book to stay safe and keep my mother and me protected. I even went so far as to educate my mother about all I had learned concerning this thing called "COVID-19"—and made sure I followed the CDC's (Centers for Disease Control and Prevention) safety precautions to the letter. The one thing I did not foresee was that my mom did not play it as safe as I have done.

I must pause to state here that I have endured a lot of situations I believe were much worse. As a child, I survived dealing with the ramifications of my mom's infidelity. I survived dealing with bullies while growing up and fighting back, only to be ostracized at times for defending myself or being lied about by them. I have survived a lot more, but I will not go there. That's another story for another time.

People think they have covered all the bases for staying safe, considering we live in the age of a global pandemic. There has not been a pandemic of this capacity since the Spanish Flu of 1918-1920. (My paternal grandmother was born during that time.)

As for my mother and me, we do not have the best relationship in the world, although she is currently my roommate (she moved in with me in July 2007). For years before and since then, things have been tense between us. My mom was never one to "play by the rules" and tended to do whatever she wanted on a regular basis. I recall when she cheated on my dad, and I called her out on it at the age of ten. Our relationship became strained and has been distant ever since. I have forgiven her for her actions, but for the most part, I know it is my duty and obligation to care for her now — **no matter what.**

So, when my mom visited with one of her friends during the 2020 Thanksgiving holiday, she thought it was just another day and let her guard down. She did not know her friend was infected with the virus. A few days later, she gets a phone call from that same friend:

"I tested positive for COVID. You better get tested."

After receiving that news, she told me she needed to get tested and suggested I do the same. The Saturday morning following Thanksgiving — November 27, 2020 — my mom took the COVID test in Riverside that her best friend's daughter had set up. She was clueless about the process. We drove through the testing line and, when it was our turn, I swabbed her mouth with the test, dropped it in the pouch, and returned home. Later that morning, I scheduled my own test in Maywood. That time, I remained in line for over two hours.

The next morning, the tip of my tongue went numb without explanation. I immediately went shopping and grabbed resources (i.e., cranberry juice, Mucinex, Dayquil/Nyquil, soups, Zinc vitamins, etc.) that my mother and I were going to need because I had a sneaky suspicion I was infected, despite all the precautions I had taken. My tongue was an indicator of what was to come. It turned out my mother was starting to show signs as well. She suffered from fatigue, cough, mucus build-up, and fluctuating sugar levels (she's a Type-2 diabetic).

Later, I went for a drive. I had to get away from my mom for a while, so I headed to my favorite secluded spot to spend time writing in my journal. I was so upset and concerned about my fate, I sat and cried for a bit. Once I pulled myself together, I then called my closest friends to let them know what happened and talked to family members as well. I honestly believed COVID was an **automatic *death* sentence**. I was genuinely fearful of what was coming but knew I had to face it head-on if I had any chance at survival.

I quickly changed my thoughts from *death* to **LIFE**. My daily prayers to God changed to include miraculous healing of my mother, aunt, and my mom's best friend.

During that time, I ensured my life maintained a sense of normalcy. I would get up at my usual time, put on my workout clothes, and exercise for about an hour. I kept praying and reading my Bible regularly. After dark, I would head to Beverly Hills to walk for about two to three miles. In the meantime, I kept a watchful eye on my mom to make sure she did not take a turn for the worst.

About four days into our quarantine, I realized I was asymptomatic—something for which I give great thanks to God. I was able to be healthy to care for my mom, cook, and help around the house. The closer I got to the end of quarantine, the more I gave thanks that I was both *alive* and *healthy*. My mom, her sister, and her best friend recuperated as well. On December 12, 2020, I got retested in Maywood. The results came back the following day: **NEGATIVE!** Life with COVID-19 is one experience I will **never** forget.

As I reflect on that time, I know everything happens for a reason. I kept the faith and my focus. I thought of **LIFE** instead of *death*—especially considering how the media regularly portrayed the ever-growing number of those who lost their battle with COVID-19.

During that time, I was able to get some writing done, stay healthy, and take care of my mom. Most importantly, I did not lose faith or hope that I was going to get through to the other side. Although my mom and I do not have the best mother/son relationship, I remain grateful that I could help her when she needed me the most. In turn, I grew from the experience and now look at the bigger picture from the lesson:

It's not about you. It's more about what **GOD** *has in store for you when it comes to your purpose and being there for others.*

Tondra "Poetic Sense" Mosley
Champion

Be as proud of the classic beauty of your past as you are eager to be the bright, successful beauty of your future, all while loving the present beauty in transition.

There is absolutely nothing wrong with striving to be the greatest **"YOU."** Truth be told, that should be your goal in life **every day**. When reaching for the greater, you may sometimes forget to appreciate the journey. You might have recklessly abandoned the good that was in your past self that you have upgraded, as if you were previously nothing to have been built upon in the first place. There is value in the person you left behind yesterday. When you remember to honor and celebrate yourself for what you conquered and survived, you realize had you not done so, you would not be standing in the gift of your **present** beauty today. You *learned* some things, *earned* some things, and *released* some things that got you to where you are today.

Then, as you look far into your future, it is as if the person you upgraded to has no value at this point. Embracing your today's self does not declare to your present that you are permanently moving in. Rather, it is that you find it beautiful enough to pay attention to it and valuable enough to enjoy and adorn it with evidence that you have arrived.

Embracing and celebrating who you are today also does not declare to your future that you are not interested in seeing its even *more beautiful self* come to pass. A significant reason to celebrate who you have become today is that when you look back at tomorrow and need strength to conquer the obstacles that are in the new day, you are going to need to know and remember what it took to get you to that place.

Celebrating who you are at every turn is LIVING!

Don't just exist while trying to get to the GREATNESS or GREATER BEAUTY you were born with!

Everything after your birth is a simple manifestation!

****

One of my favorite personal thought bombs is this:

It only takes a single fight to win the title of a **CHAMPION**. Every fight after is really about owning the rights to a piece of accessory — *'the belt.'* The belt can be taken, lost, or stolen, but you own the rights to the **TITLE** forever.

Remember: **You were** a great and beautiful CHAMPION yesterday, **you are** a great and beautiful CHAMPION today, and you **shall be** a great and beautiful CHAMPION tomorrow!

Now, accessorize your life with your **CHAMPIONSHIP BELT** and put on the whole armor of God, which includes your inner beauty!

Shglenda Green
Chasing False Love to Finding Unconditional Love

Our immediate family is commonly known as our mother, father, and siblings. Growing up, it is those individuals who we expect to love us and teach us love.

For me, I set my expectations too high.

I was abandoned by both parents—the ones who were supposed to protect me from the sexual abuse I endured by my brother from a young age until my teen years. During those challenging times, I adopted the concept of false (and failing) love.

****

As life would have it, I found myself searching for the same kind of love that was given to me. That came by way of giving my body to boys (and later, men) who I tried to gain love and acceptance from. The more I sought, the "love" I received left me feeling empty, lifeless, broken, hurt, and confused. I then started blaming my parents, brother, and the world for my brokenness.

Looking for love and acceptance in all the wrong places caused me to want a love that would be everlasting and fill my void, so at the age of 14, I told my grandmother I wanted a baby. She tried her hardest to convince me that a child was something I did not need or truly want at the time…but I didn't listen. I kept trying and trying until, at the age of 16, I conceived my first child and gave birth at the age of seventeen. I had no education nor clue about how to be a mother.

I told myself that I would be a better mom than my mother, but little did I know that although I was there with my daughter, I was still unfit. Why? Because I constantly compared myself to my mother! Before I knew it, I became like her. I slept around with anyone who told me they loved me and began indulging in recreational drugs. My parents were addicts, so it seemed like the natural progression of my life's story would lead me to that path.

During that time in my life, I exposed my daughter to an unhealthy lifestyle. The man I was with (who I thought was her father) didn't see eye-to-eye on **anything**. He was 12 years older than I — an age gap that explained our "differences." I was still a child myself and had not learned self-love, so he took advantage of that by trying to control me. One day, I got tired of his mistreatment and walked out the door…with nowhere to go. I had told myself that once I left home, I would never return.

Well…

I went back home. After a couple of months of being there, I met someone else, and we ended up getting married. That time, I was pregnant with my second child and still without a stable home, all while he was out and about living his "best life." My children and I moved from shelter to shelter and lived in my car for quite some time. There were moments when things were going well for me, which was when my husband would choose to make his reappearance. What would happen? You guessed it if you said, *"She fell into the same trap."* Time and again, my little family was left without a place to live. Then, I got pregnant…again. While still on the hunt for love and acceptance, I finally gathered the strength to divorce that man.

Although that chain was broken, I remained unhealed and continued searching for love and acceptance. I needed to do something **different**, so I searched for the man they called *"Jesus."* I attended church from time to time, but that was not enough for me. I heard what was being said but had no evidence of how my life could change or how a relationship with Jesus could work for me. Less than a year later, I remarried. Being that I was still a "babe in Christ" and trying to find my way, I didn't realize that what I needed could not be found in a man.

While in my second marriage, things were not good for me. I was depressed and about to lose my mind! Sadly, that was due to me still not knowing the difference between false and unconditional love. I failed to realize that every time I showed up in the church, the Word of God was settling in my heart. I didn't see how the Word was working in me to show me precisely what I searched for. However, little by little, I came to learn the things I did were not enough to bring me genuine joy, including how my husband called himself "showing me love." His words and actions did not line up. He was verbally abusive and played on my insecurities of lack of family (my parents and siblings were addicts, and my younger brother was incarcerated) and my brokenness. My husband took advantage of my weakness, holding me captive to my lack of self-love and not knowing what **TRUE** love was. I believed he loved me in the way I came to know love.

The Turning Point

I became Battle-Scar Free when I began to learn how to love myself and stopped allowing others to dictate who I am. The moment I stopped feeling sorry for myself and what happened to me as a child and started recognizing that what others did to me was not truly against me, my life improved significantly. I had to pray a similar prayer like the one Jesus prayed on the Cross at Calvary:

"Father, forgive them, for they know not what they do."

At every turn, it seemed as if "they" tried to destroy the plans God had for me by keeping me in an angry, bitter, selfish state of existence. I held onto resentment and unforgiveness in my heart as if my life depended on it. All those things were contrary to who God **IS**—but it took me some time to learn about His goodness, grace, and mercy for myself.

I endured many seasons of learning the differences between false and unconditional love. As I learned to follow teachings I didn't fully understand, that was when things began to change for me. That is called "walking by faith." Looking back on my life, I now see how everything that happened to me was orchestrating the day God would cause me to finally find that which I was seeking—something I could only find in **HIM**. The more I sought after God the Father and His ways, there were things I would and would not allow in my life, including being set free from the abusive marriage I was in.

Love's Lessons

When searching for love, and the search comes from emptiness and brokenness, we only find the false love given to us. In response, we embrace it and find ourselves hurting and being willing participants in the pain. Those feelings and emotions are outside of the One who created us. God is Love, and He created us out of love.

Everyone knows what love is—whether it is healthy or unhealthy. We seek a greater love than ourselves, often placing our hearts in the hands of men/women who cannot fill that empty space. We must first do what it says in Luke 10:27:

"Love the Lord your God with all your heart, and with all your soul, and with all your strength, and with all your mind; and love your neighbor as yourself."

I learned I had to first love God, despite my circumstances. I had to speak what God says about me. I confess I am a sinner. Despite who hurt me, I must release that pain and be free from bitterness, anger, and unforgiveness…one day at a time. I must love the Lord with all my soul—no matter the trial or tribulation—and allow the Holy Spirit to humble me. I had to pray the pride of life would die and continue to rise when I fall, not allowing the spirit of condemnation to set up camp in my heart and keep me down. I do all those things to this very day.

Proverbs 24:16 says, *"For though the righteous fall seven times, they rise again."* **GLORY TO GOD!**

I also learned that giving God my mind meant sharing with Him those thoughts I believed He wouldn't care about. Being very open, honest, and transparent with Him taught me intimacy with Him by allowing insight into me. Although He knew what I was dealing with, He wanted the relationship we had since the beginning of time.

For far too long, I believed it was a sin to love myself more than others, so I would tend to everyone else's needs and feel bad if I did anything for myself. That was something I was even taught in church. I didn't realize my tiredness and frustration came from me constantly giving what I did not have to offer. When I learned to love myself, I could thrive in loving my neighbor without the expectation of having that love returned. Loving myself meant learning to rid me of all the false "things" I had been living with for so long. I had to empty myself so that I could be filled with what was designed just for me.

"Blessed are those who hunger and thirst for righteousness, for they will be filled" (Matthew 5:6).

When you come to understand that false love is keeping you bound to those things that will stunt your freedom, you will experience an unconditional love that does not change. That love will wait for you with open arms to receive you in the warmest embrace. Then, you can be made whole and, in turn, give love to another to help them experience freedom from death to life, especially if they are in a place where there seems to be no hope.

When true love flourishes in your life, nothing artificial can withstand love's power. True unconditional love comes with an assurance:

"...that their hearts may be encouraged, having been knit together in love, and attaining to all the wealth that comes from the full assurance of understanding resulting in true knowledge of God's mystery, that is, Christ Himself" (Colossians 2:2).

Being able to walk in the complete victory of who you are and *who's* you are is everything! The only way I could become Battle-Scar Free was by trying something other than the ways of the world. I have life, and I truly have it more abundantly, even when I'm going through. That is because I now have a love that **NEVER** fails, surrounds me, and is in me. Therefore, because of this love, I can give love to others without conditions placed on it. Most importantly, I have stopped allowing false love from entering through the doors of my heart.

Nikki Denise
From 13 to 30-Something, I am Battle-Scar Free

What battle-scars do you have that you need to seek God's guidance for during your valley experiences? Life will give you many challenges, tests, and trials that become testimonies. It is not uncommon to be unsure of the reasons you must endure. The purpose of this writing is to share with you some of my life's experiences and to advocate for others by helping them to understand that although they are scarred, healing is possible. To everyone reading this, understand the scars of life teach us about building our faith.

"Now, faith is the substance of things hoped for, the evidence of things not seen." (Hebrews 11:1)

You will acquire various scars from many types of abusive 'situations' in your lifetime. Do not shy away from your hardships. When they come, your inner strength will be what allows them to begin the healing process. The key to understanding how to overcome is to develop a prayer life with **GOD.** Never settle for less than what His Word says concerning you. Stand firm in your faith because that is what will always carry you each time a battle-scar becomes part of your life's story.

My Battle-Scar Free Testimony

Admittedly, I have overcome many challenges, trials, and tests in my life that were designed to destroy me. Over the years, I have experienced divorce, sexual abuse, emotional abuse, mental abuse, and abandonment. Each battle-scar has served to stretch me to learn who **GOD** says I am. There were times in my life when I wanted to quit…give up…throw in the towel, **BUT GOD'S** will for my life would not allow them to come to pass. Be encouraged, my friend, in knowing this: God will send you people or things that give you the power to be an overcomer.

The worst abuse I experienced was when I was raped at the age of 13 by a family member. *My God…* At that age, I was precious, young, and so full of life. That instance of sexual abuse served to shape my world into a place of brokenness. Still, through it all, I maintained my closeness to **GOD**. The man who assaulted me said that if I ever told, he would kill me (the common threat of pedophiles). I was left with the "scars" of his nasty, stinky face and hands, along with the memories of how he penetrated my innocence. Just the recollection makes me sick to the core. Even at that young age, I could not fathom how someone could be sick-minded enough to take advantage of a child — of *ME* — at such a tender time in life.

For years, I held tight to the battle-scar of being raped. I grew up without understanding how it was possible for me to do so. Each day, I questioned my self-worth, self-esteem, and self-value. Who was Nikki Denise? It seemed it did not matter because "she" was stolen from "me." I lived a life of confusion and uncertainty, which was not helped by being abandoned by my mother when she simply gave me to my grandmother so that she could seek help for her own mental illness. My father was not the man he should have been, leaving me to experience different trials with men because I was not taught about the opposite sex properly.

As a result of what I did not know but accepted as my norm, many days felt as if I were living in Hell's hottest fire. The scars of life had seemingly settled deep into my bones. No one had a clue about what was happening inside of my mind, body, and spirit. Having to keep "the secret" for years had proven horrible for my psyche. There were times when I bathed, the recollection of my rapist on top of me would cause me to have a panic attack. I had to remind myself that there was nothing too hard from which God can deliver me.

Many of life's lessons cost me dearly before I truly learned them and was able to overcome by following God's plan and knowing what He required of me through an active prayer life. It took strength, reading the Word of God, and understanding that I was **ALL** He said He created me to be. I also had the praying spirit of my grandmother on my side. She knew something evil was upon my heart, and she kept me close to her each day.

When I was 35 years old, I was a single mother of a young son. I began dating a man who took me through some tumultuous trials and tests in my life—ones that would have broken the spirit of many women or men. The man I loved mentally abused me to no end. He was disrespectful and talked down to me after drinking or being influenced by other negative mindsets. Nonetheless, I married him (a marriage that should have never happened). Because I did not obey the commandments God had placed before me concerning my life, I had to learn "the hard way" and on my own.

NOTE: The most significant lessons in life are the ones we repeat until we eventually learn not to do them again. It is in that place when we discover the truth of who we are. Only then can we help others and show them how to be in alignment with God's plan.

Mental abuse is described as *"a form of abuse that disrupts the brain's actual flow of being able to think and process information."* As such, when someone is mentally abusive, it will cause their victim to believe those things spoken to and about them. I liken it to an evil force controlling the brain's section that processes that "information." (Be sure to practice self-love during those times. You must surround yourself with people who will uplift you and help to defeat the enemy's tricks. Know there is **nothing** God will not do for you.)

Please adhere to this advice: When your past pains or scars come to mind, speak **HEALING** and **LIFE** over those emotions and thoughts. They have no Heaven or Hell to place you into, so denounce them by the spirit of God's love, grace, and mercy. Remember that Christ is greater than *ALL* things. We must teach people how to treat us. Take a stand for yourself. On this journey called "life," everything has value — whether it is to teach, strengthen, stretch, or educate. Love will always surpass everything that happens in life because love conquers all things.

Following are some scripture references that may help guide you when you encounter challenging moments:

- ❖ 1 Samuel 15:22
- ❖ Psalms 30:2

- ❖ Proverbs 3:5-6
- ❖ Matthew 11:28; 25:21
- ❖ Mark 9:23
- ❖ Luke 17:11-19

In times of trouble, you can call on the name of God or go into praise and worship, which will always confuse the 'author of confusion' (Satan). The Word of God tells us the thief (the devil) comes to steal, kill, and destroy but that God comes that we may have life to the fullest (see John 10:10). When I face obstacles in my life, those powerful words keep my mind focused on healing my battle-scars.

Life will educate you on how to win beyond purpose. It will teach you what is right from wrong and, along the way, make way for your scars to heal. **Remember:** Healing comes from working hard to help yourself heal. I pray the sharing of my story will help others who might be dealing with traumatic scarring and that they understand God's children are healed by His stripes and set free from those scars. The lessons I learned along the way were hardcore, challenging, and priceless. I had to know within my soul that my battle-scars were, indeed, freed from the pains of the past.

God tells us His strength is made perfect in anything. What you believe will always overpower what your natural eyes see. Do not run away from the giant storms that come during your journey. Embrace every attack, lesson, and teaching moment because they will grow faith in your abilities to become a better "you." You are not placed on this earth to live confined to a corner. You have a purpose: to fulfill God's promises by what His Word says about your life. It may help you always to remember that life is a vapor, and you must live each day knowing what was designed just for you. Move mountains out of the way by staying in prayer and remaining focused on how to purge your heart from the scars that hinder your growth. Always give yourself permission to become a better you. Release those things that tried to break you. Mount up like an eagle that soars and wait for God to say, *"NOW!"* Then, give Him thanks.

Today, you can now allow your hurts, past pains, and battle-scar wounds of old to be set free from walking into the presence of your greatness! God has ordered your footsteps, and your new journey for the next level can begin. You are now released to be **BATTLE-SCAR FREE!**

A Prayer for Greater Joy

Lord, fill me with Your grace and mercy that is sufficient daily. Everything You have placed inside of me will continue to shine through me as I walk with You. Father, I ask today that Your Word continue to stand boldly before the masses. As each challenge from my past battle-scars come upon me, teach me Thy ways, Lord. Allow me to talk and walk like You, for You are the God of second chances. Purge me daily, O Lord, for Your love is always beyond my perceived value and worth. Stand before the way of the wicked hearts of others and create in them a clean heart, right mind, and spirit of forgiveness. Lord, there is nothing nor no one like You, for acknowledging who You are truly allows Your saving grace to surpass all understanding. I love You, Lord. There is none greater. Thank You for saving a wretch like me. May the peace and love of Your Kingdom stand solely over my life forever and always.

Amen.

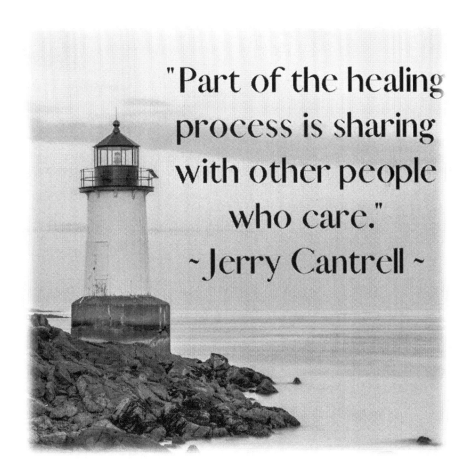

Nakia Allen
Free from Pleasing People

"Am I now trying to win the approval of human beings or God? Or am I trying to please people? If I were still trying to please people, I would not be a servant of Christ." (Galatians 1:10)

When I think about being **Battle-Scar Free**, I think about what it took to **become** *Battle-Scar Free*. My life's journey has always been somewhat of a struggle. I was raised by a strong, orderly, and strict single woman who taught me how to carry myself a certain way. I always had to "look right," "talk right," and "act right." My mother was no one to play with.

Growing up in that type of environment made me very self-conscious. As I got older, I found that I concentrated more on my outer-self than my inner-self. Now, don't get me wrong: I truly appreciate and love my mother for making me the woman I am today. It is, after all, for mothers to train up their young ladies to behave like ladies. Mothers are also tasked with teaching them the merits of obeying their parents and trusting their inner voice.

The problem comes when we start letting the opinions of others matter more than God's opinion.

My battle began when I got married at a young age. I met my then-husband, fell in love, and married him right away. I recall him asking me to marry him on a Friday, and the next day, we were newlyweds. Some would say I started the marriage off "wrong" because my parents were not in attendance, but I didn't have the time to let them know because my husband wanted to get married so quickly. Honestly, I did not want to disappoint him or his family, so I agreed to the arrangement, and we got married during a choir rehearsal. My mother didn't speak to me for a month.

In the blink of an eye, I left my mother's home to live with my new husband. I had plans to live on my own first, but things moved so fast that I completely forgot about my intentions. I was young and excited about being someone's wife—although I didn't know how to *be* one.

A single woman raised me, so I found myself clinging to my husband's mother because she was a wife and made it look easy. She was my "Naomi," and I was her "Ruth." Her people were my people. Where she led, I followed. I remember following her to church one Sunday, and it changed my life forever. I loved the feeling of being accepted by God and His people. That following Sunday, I joined her church. Then, I joined every team I could, including the dance team, intercessory team, and the praise and worship team. I even joined the youth leadership team! I wanted that feeling of being accepted **EVERY** day. I attended church so much, my family started complaining about me being there more than at home!

As the years progressed, my people-pleasing grew while I ignored the things I wanted and needed. At one point, my husband was a Youth Minister, and I worked with him in the youth ministry. I didn't always agree with how he and his family ran the ministry, but I never spoke out of turn concerning my true feelings because I didn't want to be out of order or looked upon as being rebellious.

All the while, I continued to ignore that small voice in my head that screamed, *"THIS IS NOT THE FREE LIFE GOD PROMISED ME!"*

As life would have it, my marriage started to deteriorate. I was in church **ALL** the time, and my husband worked every weekend. His complaints about me being in church more than at home started to wear on me. I just wanted a normal life. We were both young and wanted to do what "normal" young people did — and still please our church family.

At one point during our marriage, my husband started dating a young lady on his job. When I found out, I approached the elder ladies in the church. I was a young mother of two boys at the time and needed guidance. One of the ladies said to me, *"Do not give another woman what you have already trained."* Another said, *"You need to give him more sex."* **Sigh**. I received a *lot* of advice that day.

What I really needed was some time alone to think, but I didn't listen to my inner voice. Instead, I took their advice…and stayed married for 15 years, all while dealing with more than my fair share of his infidelity. My heart and spirit were broken. I had truly lost my identity. I didn't know who I was without my family. Fear had paralyzed me. Although I was going to church regularly, I wasn't trusting in God's Word. I was merely going through the motions of life.

One day, I just got tired of the same old pace and decided to fast for a month. I didn't tell anyone, deciding to take God at His Word where He says that some things are not moved except by fasting and prayer. During my last week of fasting, my husband and I got into a huge argument—something he often instigated, just to find a reason to do whatever he wanted. I was tired of his antics. That night, I wrote three things in my journal that I needed to be able to live **without** my husband:

1. A better job that paid more.
2. A new place to live.
3. My car paid off.

I immediately began working on those three goals, and God blessed me with accomplishing them **ALL** in the same year.

Once I got my own place, my new life consisted of living without my husband, my church family, and even my friends. Life was different and challenging. I spent a lot of nights second-guessing myself, even as I relied solely on God's provisions and promises…and my abilities. I had to learn how to trust myself and God's Word.

During that time, I realized I didn't have a close, *personal* relationship with God. Something had to change — and it did! I promised God and myself that whenever something didn't feel right, it wasn't right for me and that I would trust that small inner voice.

It has been a long journey, and I have a long way to go. Nonetheless, I am grateful for everything that has happened. Time has made me able to forgive and even have a friendship with my ex-husband. I have learned so many things along the way and gained the tools needed to help me live the life I desire. Today, I am **FREE** from other people's opinions of me. I now know this journey I am on is not one in which I walk alone, for God is *always* with me. **I've been freed from the battle!**

I shared this piece of my testimony to help someone who is living their life trusting in "man" instead of God. I encourage you to trust God's voice and spend time alone with Him so that you will know what His voice sounds like. It worked for me, and it will work for you. He is not a respecter of person. What He does for me, He will do for **YOU**, too! *Live Battle-Scar Free!*

Laurie Benoit
This Was the Story of a Broken Girl

Childhood.
Notably, it is the most crucial time of development in every person's life.

amily is usually the very first key to the road a person travels in life. *Family* is the very foundation of how **YOU**, as a person, treat everyone else who you come across for the entirety of your life. Those very first *familial* relationships generally set the trend for all others that follow.

When you reflect on your childhood, what do you recall? What kinds of memories does your life entail? Was it filled with love, hugs, birthday parties, moments baking with mom, cuddles with grandparents, playing with dad, and fun family celebrations? Maybe you had some of those moments, but not all — or maybe…just *MAYBE* your childhood was like mine.

*I honestly wish I could say I had **any** of those things, but I cannot.*

I have **NEVER** revealed the full depths of my childhood, **EXCEPT** to those I believed could help me so many years ago.

Sadly, everything I shared was ultimately dismissed because my "group" of abusers repeatedly called **ME** *"A Liar."*

Honestly, I believe wholeheartedly that label—being called a *liar* and constantly accused of *lying*—has angered me so much throughout the years. Even when I, too, know I have been guilty of lying to others, it has been something that has gnawed away at my soul like a deep, seething **rot**, eating away at the flesh of my very being.

The abuse happened many years ago, but it is still as fresh in my mind as when it all began—at least the horrors I can *remember*.

Our family celebrations were nothing like what one would expect or hope for, but they definitely made a lasting impression on my life. In fact, I almost always dreaded family get-togethers because we never knew what kind of visit we would have. The visits weren't always horrifying, but more often than not, they were. It really depended on with whom we spent our time.

It is because of those gatherings that I know I display signs of Dissociative Amnesia and Post-Traumatic Stress

Disorder (PTSD), even though I have never been officially diagnosed with either condition.

Incest.

My childhood entailed some of the worst possible scenarios you could imagine revolving around incest and molestation. It seemed no one was exempt.

Father? *Check.*
Stepmother? *Check.*
Brother? *Check.*
Aunts? *Check.*
Uncles? *Check.*
Grandparents? *Check.*

For many years, I never realized why I felt such a heaviness and terror within my so-called "family." Why did I always feel as if I never belonged? Why were my nightmares so dark? Where were the years of my life that were completely void?

As I grew older, some of the sickening rituals I endured and recalled refused to be blocked from my memory. In fact, some of them have literally opened the *"Gates of Hell"* and made way for other memories — ones that have replayed like a broken record that repeatedly skipped *over* and *over* and *over* again...

When regular beatings, spiritual abuse, emotional abuse, gaslighting, scapegoating, and neglect are added, they become the recipe for what? I'll tell you: **A person who could go either way in life.** At times, I am sure it would have been easier to embrace the abuse (in some type of twisted manner) and become the subservient child "they" hoped to condition. Perhaps I should have allowed the sickness to overtake me and make excuses for their actions as those before me had done. Instead, I fought with every ounce of my being to stand and say something. I needed to overcome all the horrors I should have never had to endure.

From somewhere deep within, even as young children, we must develop our own sense of self-preservation and strong moral standing. But where do those feelings come from when we are trying to *grow* through such a tumultuous life?

I really cannot explain how I knew those behaviors were not right. I just *knew*. Truthfully, I'm not certain when the abuse and incest began, but I vividly recall being very young. In the confines of the two-story home with the narrow stairwell where I resided, I would clench the bars of my crib with all my might and scream in terror as if my very life depended on it…*because it did.* Someone had been in my room, but the memory of who and why is unclear. I just remember screaming those blood-curdling screams.

Why, as such a young child, was I so terrified? Why is that memory engraved into my mind like a carving etched in stone?

The fact is this: That is the **very first** memory I have of my life. Why I remember it still so clearly all these years later baffles me, for along with that recollection, I also vaguely recall my very young brother quietly trying to comfort and quiet me.

As he and I grew through our childhood, I carried a heaviness and terror within me, and I could never truly understand why. There were plenty of times — even in my very youngest of years — that I remember the overwhelming feeling of fear, causing me to run away somewhere to hide. It was not until I started getting older that I realized just what was happening to us…not just to **ME**, but to ***US***.

I suppose I can be grateful that a good portion of those memories is still blocked from my mind. After all, would I really want to remember them? Probably not. The ones I do recall are enough to bring me to tears and give me night terrors even now.

To provide a little backstory: My birth parents divorced when I was so young, I didn't remember my biological mother at all (I am certain my sister's death may have played an integral role in their divorce, although I cannot say for sure). I am not in contact with either of my birth parents, but if I had to guess, I would imagine my train of thought is accurate. In fact, thoughts of my sister's death have plagued my mind throughout the years, as she "apparently" died before I was born. I have been told she passed away from SIDS (Sudden Infant Death Syndrome), but somewhere in the pit of my stomach, I have a really difficult time believing that to be the truth. It is challenging to accept the word of someone who neglected me for long periods throughout my life or, worse yet, that of ones who abused me so harshly, it has taken me a lifetime to attempt to heal from it all. Imagine my surprise when I ordered my own legal documents (including my birth registration), and they stated my sister was still **alive** at the time of my birth!

It would have been nice to have an older sister. Perhaps my life would have been different with her presence. Nonetheless, she is not here now. Admittedly, it is probably for the best, as she is one less person in my "birth family" who cannot harm another…or *me*.

As far back as I can remember, "family" visits were an important piece of my life. The reasons for them, though, were disturbingly sick in ritual. Yes, a few good memories were mixed in with the horrors inflicted upon us, but I'm sure those "good times" were there to **TRY** to mask what was happening behind closed doors.

Visits with my paternal grandparents always made me feel uncomfortable. My grandmother would consistently call me into her room, where she would be only half-dressed. She would then nestle my face into her chest, all while trying to pretend she was showing me affection. Well, it was affection…*just not the type I cared for.* Thankfully, she never fully revealed her body to me.

On the other hand, my grandfather would pretend to "play" with me, all while groping my young body. He would act as if he were tickling me, but I knew what he was doing. If I recall correctly, I was always alone with them in private rooms when those instances took place.

Then, there were the "summer family holidays" with my father, stepmother, stepmother's sister, and her husband at a lodge. I always hated those visits because there was usually what I now understand to be an *orgy* between all of them. My brother and I were expected to watch, as well as partake — sometimes together, and other times only one of us at any given time. There were also visits and holidays with "friends of the family" that would entail the same types of behaviors.

What really sickens me is that my birth family carries an attitude of perfection, an abundance of narcissism, and the belief that they are of pedigree descent. Sadly, they are things I never believed. In fact, it is because of my noncompliance to accept them as truth that my family has scapegoated me. Imagine my satisfaction the day I no longer had to carry the "family name" — one I will **never** reclaim, no matter where my journey in life takes me.

At one point in my life, I very vividly remember my stepmother being away from home. I'm not sure about my exact age at the time, but I was told my father and she were on the verge of getting a divorce because of *ME*. Was there any truth to that? I do not know with any level of surety. Honestly, I believe their "separation" was a way for my father to take advantage of and have his way with me. It was during that time when the molestation peaked. For days (maybe even weeks), I promised him I would be a better child, if only he would leave *her*. The more I pleaded, the more sexual abuse I endured.

The sight of my father repulsed me then, and even now, just the **thought** of him still does. He also made certain to tell me he *never* wanted me to perform specific sexual acts with anyone else. Believe me: Those 'things' I have *never* done. My PTSD kicks into overdrive, and I literally get physically ill by the mere **thought** of those 'things.'

And so, as abruptly as my stepmother left, she made her reappearance — *and all hell broke loose!* It was as if my father told her **everything** that I said about wishing she were gone because, from that point, the physical abuse became more aggressive. In fact, I spent more time out of school than in during that time because of the beatings I suffered.

I recall one of the nights while my father and stepmother went to the bar in town, I was left alone at home with my brother. My formerly "protective" brother forced himself on me. Yes, my brother raped me. Afterward, he tried to soothe me by offering me a piece of the freshly made pie that sat on the kitchen counter. We both indulged and then went to bed. Sometime later, I was teetering on the edge of sleep when…

I was suddenly yanked out of bed by my hair while simultaneously being beaten with a boot jack. The assailant was my stepmother. She dragged and beat me all the way into the kitchen. Once there, she stood me up by my hair and asked me about the missing piece of the pie. My brother looked up at me from the place where he was seated at the table and said, *"Just tell them the truth that you ate the pie. You're not going to be in as much trouble."* **Yeah…right!** We both knew the truth about what he did to me earlier that evening that led to the missing piece of the pie, yet I **still** wanted to protect him.

So, to keep my brother out of as much trouble as I knew I faced, I took the blame—and the pie plate right in my face. By then, the bruises from the boot jack beating were beginning to show, and my nose had just been broken. Two black eyes, a broken nose, and black and blue bruising from head to toe were my lot that night…

The next day, the school was called and told I would not be in for a matter of days because I was "ill." Thankfully, my father and stepmother still went to work. So, for as long as it took, I waited until they left, put on the loosest fitting clothes I had, and slowly hobbled my way to the police station, which was almost on the other side of town. I needed to make a report with my "evidence." The police questioned me, took pictures of my injuries, and then (much to my horror) called my stepmother (of all people!) to meet us at our home.

What I endured next was *unfathomable*...

As soon as the doors closed and the police left, out came the boot jack again. That time, she wailed on me from my neck down to my feet, hitting me as violently as she could with all her might. The difference that time was that she also began spewing out all the things she probably always wanted to say to me. The beating was so harsh, I passed out from the pain. When I came to, she was seated beside me in a chair. I was forced to get up and into the bath of ice water she had prepared to aid with bringing down the swelling. How I managed to get in and out of the tub eludes my memory. That very day, she told me, *"If you ever do that again, you will **never** set foot outside the house again."* I believed every word she spoke with every ounce of my being.

What no one knew was that deep down, I decided I'd had enough. I started making plans to run away—with or without my brother. I knew I was no longer safe at home nor in town. Heck, I doubted my police report was ever filed! The time came when I had to do something drastic that would get *someone's* attention!

I'm not sure how long it was before I ran, but it hadn't been long, for I still had bruises covering my entire body. I do recall that I was caught at school within a few days of my grand escape while trying to get warm and change my clothes. And because I was in the school when I got caught, the principal was permitted to hit me with the strap for being **"A Liar"** when I tried to divulge to the administrators about the abuse I had recently endured. *(Apparently, my two black eyes weren't enough proof...)*

Can you guess what happened next? Yes, **another** beating by stepmom.

I made preparations to run away again—only that time, I was a bit more prepared and planned to contact Child Protection Services. I desperately wanted OUT, and time was not on my side! *If only I could get somewhere safe and, perhaps, get my brother out, too...*

I didn't anticipate that even though my life would change, it wouldn't change much.

Enter in the foster care system.

After years spent in foster care, I reencountered my brother, but our relationship was never the same. In fact, after we both had grown into adulthood, we had a tremendous falling out and have had no contact since. What was the disagreement, you ask?

Well…

My brother decided that remaining in contact with both sides of our family would earn him riches and wealth by proving his loyalty. I, on the other hand, decided my sanity was not for sale.

Years after I lost contact with him, I read in the news that he had been charged with rape. After a year in custody, he appealed — and the charges were overturned! Was he guilty? In my mind, I believe so…without a shadow of a doubt. If he can rape his own flesh and blood, why not someone else?

I have since vowed to steer my life in the furthest possible direction *away* from the strongholds of generational sickness and abuse. I eventually met a man who became my loving husband. He allowed me to heal without judgment and has supported me as I work to overcome all that I endured in life. I am also appreciative of his encouragement as I use my own words to rebuild my life through my literary journey.

Not so long ago, I began writing about my experiences to give healing, offer hope, and inspire change in others. From that journey, I am learning to become more and more **BATTLE-SCAR FREE!**

Angela R. Edwards

Craig Mosley, Sr.
Why Me?

Why **ME**? Why is this happening to **ME**? Why did others choose to make the decision for **ME** about how **MY** life should be? Why must I be confused about **MY** sexuality?

At a young age, I spent some time in the foster care system. I often wonder if I was getting touched on by another child or adult in the home. I wasn't there for long because my grandmother got me out of there and eventually reunited me with my parents. Sadly, I became a target of molestation by several people I trusted — ones who **should have** protected me from harm.

When in school, people often called me "gay" because I had some feminine ways and was not "thuggish" like the other boys. What really hurt me to my very soul was when my mother called me a "fag" (although I am sure she would never admit to doing so). I have a witness, though. She called me a fag in front of my girlfriend at the time. *Really, mom?* ***Really?***

One thing about me is this: I don't easily forget things that truly *HURT* me. Perhaps that's my downfall...

I also remember one of my molesters having the nerve to say to me, *"You're acting like a girl."* That comment came amid an argument between the two of us. In my head, I screamed, ***"How dare you! After knowing what you have been doing to me since the age of seven until I became a teen!"***

The Guilt

At some point, I started getting used to the abuse, although I knew what was happening to me wasn't right. There were late-night visits to my room when I was scared out of my sleep by "HIM" doing ungodly things to me, including urinating on me.

Far too many times to count, I asked myself questions countless victims of molestation pose: Why do I feel guilty about being molested? Why did I continue to let the abuse occur? Why did I protect them and not let someone know what was happening to me?

I know the all-encompassing answer to those questions: I was **TOO** ashamed, **TOO** confused…and **TOO** embarrassed.

The Confusion

What kind of body language was I displaying that made "HIM" and other people do those things to me? What was I doing to make men want me? Why was I more feminine than my peers?

I used to hate myself for a long time for acting that way.

In the 11th and 12th grades, I decided to see a doctor to be prescribed antidepressant medication because I was dealing with suicidal thoughts. I was tired of people thinking I was gay and judging me, all without knowing what was happening to me behind closed doors. I know I wasn't "born gay," so just where did it all begin?

The Pain

I never liked being called a fag and totally despised how people *assumed* I was gay.

Why didn't my parents see that something was wrong with me? Why didn't they question my femininity and take me to talk to a professional to find the root cause of my issues? Why couldn't they see that their baby boy was hurting and contemplating suicide?

This situation has caused me to lose my first love and my family in my adult life because I never fully dealt with healing from a lifetime of abuse. The same wounds have affected my wife and children due to my decision to face the struggle alone.

I left our home because I knew I was really sick. It wasn't fair to my wife for me to stay while I battled the demons.

For a long time, I kept all that I had gone through to myself. Now, I'm trying to let it all go.

The Release

How can I let go of something I started to enjoy? How can I release that "thing" that became a part of **ME**?

Even though I know what I feel is wrong, I often find myself crying out to the Lord, *"Deliver me, in the name of Jesus! Free me from captivity! Loose these chains! Free my soul so that I can do Your will for my life!"*

I sing praises to God and pray, knowing my deliverance is coming soon. I truly believe that before I die, I will be **FREE** and (hopefully) remarried. I would love a second chance at getting it right.

In the meantime, I'm going to continue giving God praise and glory until the day I leave this earth. Yes, I still struggle with my past, but I have repented and asked God to help me resist the desire. One day *SOON*, I will be **Battle-Scar Free!**

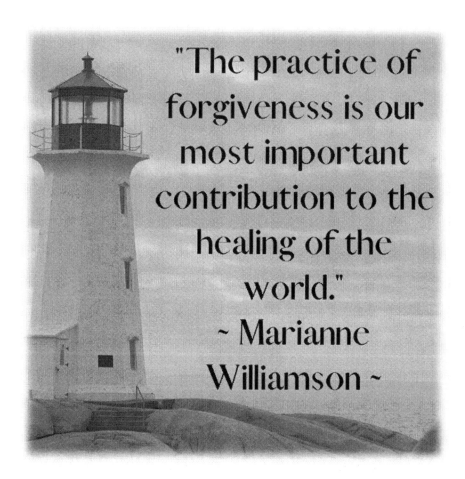

God Says I am Battle-Scar Free – Part Seven

Alexandra Esperance
Black Heart - A Poem

Black Heart. That's what I have.
Eleven, young, beautiful, and brown.
Trying to figure out what's real and what's not.
Being confused about "good touch" and "bad touch."

Like a dog being muzzled, I stay silent.
I close my eyes, hoping that would help it end,
Only to hear him moan and grunt.
My body froze, unable to feel my senses,
As he whispered, "Don't tell anyone."
My mind searches for someone,
Yet there was no one to tell.
The voices in my head taunted me:
"They won't believe you, anyway."
I ponder, "Is this what love means?"

Letting my secret encounter control my life,
I swallow…hard.
Swallow after swallow,
My throat turns into a sponge.
With each one, my throat expands.
It tightens — It's swelling — I'm gasping for air!
I lay across the bathroom floor,
Hoping my pain will end.
The salty tears stain my face,
Just like he tainted my heart…
My Black Heart.

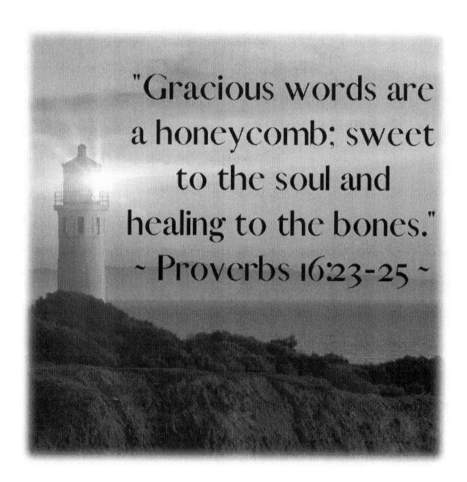

Tosha R. Dearbone
Rejection Could Have Killed Me

Just when I thought it was over, they showed up again. To what am I referring? The thoughts, the emotions, and the unbelief that I am not good enough.

As I sat on the side of my bed, I could feel each of those emotions begin to stir within me as the tears rolled down my face. The **shame**... The **fear**... I asked myself, *"**WHY?** Why do people continue coming into my life, acting as if they love and care for me, when all along, they display no true value of any good thing?"* Ohhhh, the *fakeness* of it all! Yes, there were the periodic conversations and times when they reached out to me, but most of the time, I was ignored as if I did not exist. Could they make it any clearer that the connections were left dangling open just so they could get whatever they wanted from me?

It was then when I began to see big red letters flash in my mind:

GASLIGHTING

Gaslighting is a form of emotional abuse that is often seen in abusive relationships. It is the act of manipulating a person by forcing them to question their thoughts, memories, and the events occurring around them.

In my case, it started to become more relevant because not only was I experiencing it as an adult, but it also showed up when I was a young girl...*and I did not know it.*

Come with me on my journey...

You see, growing up, I always felt the need to make myself noticeable around our home because my mom worked at night, and during the day, her presence was slim to none. Most often, I was left at home with my brothers, who were doing their own thing, so them recognizing that I was even around was a joke. (I could not be upset with them for that, though, because they were boys.) Whenever one of them held any form of conversation with me at any time, it made me feel valued. Still, I disliked the fact that they would receive most of my mom's attention when she was home.

Then, there were times I would be around my friends, and I found myself comparing their parent/child relationships to my mother/daughter one. The feeling of emptiness in my life was all-encompassing. At every turn, I would latch on to their families as if they were my own. Yep! I was trying to fit in where I could get in. When one of my friends disowned me without an explanation after I got pregnant in high school, it set me back. Rejection had reared its ugly head yet again!

Did **anyone** care for me? Did **anyone** want to be around me? Mixed emotions flooded my very soul. I began to have higher anxiety levels, frequent thoughts of suicide, and the feelings of rejection overwhelmed me—all attributed to those I loved. Talk about pain! That pain would set me off any time someone would pretend they had time for me but did the complete opposite after getting whatever it was that they needed from me.

Learning about rejection in my 30s was not something I had considered up to that point in my life. That's right, my friend. **GASLIGHTING** led to *REJECTION*.

"In the field of mental health care, rejection most frequently refers to the feelings of shame, sadness, or grief people feel when they are not accepted by others. [For example], a person might feel rejected after a significant other ends a relationship." (goodtherapy.org)

When I started doing some soul-searching, I discovered the seeds of rejection and abandonment began at the age of seven after my dad's passing. That day, I did not make it to the hospital in time to say goodbye. No one talked about him much after that day, so my feelings got shoved underneath a rug. That was until…

One day, my brother and I were arguing, at which time he blurted out:

"THAT'S WHY YOUR DAD DIED OF AIDS!"

Wait. What? Wow! I was so hurt, lost, and confused because I was told my dad passed away from complications associated with pneumonia (I later learned his AIDS diagnosis was attributed to a blood transfusion).

That moment in time — the argument with my brother — has never left my mind. It proved to add more fuel to the fire that let me know my own brothers saw me as an enemy. I was someone they did not care much for and would do anything they could to hurt me. Why would I discern something like that from one profound moment in time?

Well...

Abuse was no hidden thing around my neck of the woods. As a little girl, I sometimes dreamt about my dad being shot behind our apartments. In the dream, I could see who shot him and precisely where he was shot. As I got older, the dream became more vivid and showed my dad and stepfather (my mother and stepfather were not married at the time) in a dispute involving my mom when the gun went off. In my dream, I could hear the commotion and the siren blaring from the ambulance, and could see a puddle of blood where my father lay. From that day, the dream would not go away.

Instead, it made me sad some nights, and I would cry myself to sleep.

What hurts me most is that I do not have many memories of my dad. One of the most prominent is when I was sexually abused at his apartment by a cousin when I was left in his care while my dad went to the store.

Moving forward…

As the years went by, I witnessed my brothers arguing and fighting with their girlfriends. When I had enough, I called the police one day. I just knew what my brother was doing was not right (I am sure that incident put additional strain on our relationship, but right is right and wrong is wrong). I was called out of my name throughout my youth and told things I knew were both unkind and untrue about me. Although I was introduced to emotional and verbal abuse in the home while growing up, I never suspected physical abuse would be my lot.

In 1997, physical abuse entered my life without realizing the journey was just beginning. From one relationship to the next, I was hit, slapped, choked, ran off the road, and even had a gun put to my head. When I told my mom about all that was happening to me, her response was simply, *"He won't do it again."* I began to feel like she did not care and that the abuse must have been normal, so I would fight back and make up afterward as if nothing even happened.

It took me years to realize the rejection, abuse, and suicide attempts (yes, there were multiple) all pointed back to the fact that those I loved the most were actually demonstrating they were battling with their own secrets—ones of abuse, death, abandonment, fear, lack of love, and more. Being that that was the case, how could they show me genuine love and concern? The answer is plain. They **couldn't**. I recall asking my mom, *"How come I can forgive everyone so easily?"* —to which she replied, *"I don't know because I can't!"*

Perhaps my mother harbored ill feelings toward me because I got pregnant at the ages of 15 and 16, and she was embarrassed. It is not like I was *trying* to get pregnant. I was not thinking about the consequences of having unprotected sex because I was searching for the love I desperately wanted and needed. Sadly, the result of my "search" was that I was only people-pleasing—something I did with everyone. Acceptance was so important to me.

Fast forward…

In 2018, there was a moment when I wanted to commit suicide so badly due to that ugly friend of mine— **REJECTION**—showing up again. I remember walking around my room, not thinking about anyone or anything else outside of the idea that if I just 'disappeared,' it would all be over. No one would have to worry about me (not as if they already did).

I must pause my story for just a moment to say this: Don't get me wrong. My children cared a lot about me, but it was my mom and brothers who I wanted just to *notice* me, have *conversations* with me, and *spend time* with me. I was always left out. I never received invites for a visit. Heck, I did not even know where my brothers lived because I was not "important enough" to know!

So, there **REJECTION** was, uninvited and showing up with people who said they were my friends. Before I knew it, rejection's hold had taken total control—its force being so powerful, I could not see past what it was doing to me.

On that dreadful day, when I contemplated suicide, I paced back and forth with my overwhelming thoughts while recalling triggering moments. At one point, I even envisioned my own death and found myself asking, *"Will my family even show up to my funeral?"*

Crazy. I know.

Well, **GOD** had a different plan for my life. **HE** laughed at me while I kept questioning Him: *"Why do YOU want to keep*

ME?" Perhaps His laughter subsided a tad as I cried out to Him in earnest, *"You know these people can't stand me. I have four children and no help from their fathers. My oldest daughter's harsh words of, 'I don't like you,' continue to ring loudly in my head. My brother's messages telling me, 'Nobody's going to want you with four kids,' seems to be ringing true. My mom is completely disconnected from me. My other brother's distasteful words of death burn my soul: 'You should have died when you hit your head on that table.' So, I ask again, Lord:* **WHY DO YOU WANT TO KEEP ME HERE?!!!"**

I recall hearing his response loud and clear through His laughter:

"I HAVE WORK FOR YOU TO DO."

Work?! Was He serious?! Of course, His reply made **NO** sense to me at that moment, but now — in 2021 — things are much clearer. The vision God gave me in 2014 was bigger than anything I could have imagined. He gives us eyes to see and ears to hear, so I first needed to see what God was showing me, listen to His voice, and picture myself doing the work — **HIS** work and the process to get me there: **Vision, Envision, and Whole.**

Vision – The faculty or state of being able to see.

Envision – Imagine as a future possibility; visualize.

Whole - A coherent system or organization of parts fitting or working together as one [emotionally, spiritually, and physically].

At the dawning of 2021, I was reminded of the process…both the good and the bad. I was **ALSO** reminded about my faith in God and that REJECTION COULD NOT KILL ME—no matter what. Instead, it gave me the strength to persevere and be a vessel to help young ladies and women to realize they are enough. **WE** are enough.

I share my story in hopes that you, too, will recognize your worth and the value of God's hand on your life. Allow yourself time to process your hurt feelings. Get to know yourself and forgive. Grant forgiveness to yourself without looking for or expecting an apology from another. Why? Because you might be waiting for an apology that will never come. Please do not remain stuck in aimless thoughts of unworthiness. Be open to receiving the true meaning of **FREEDOM**.

"For I am convinced that neither death nor life, neither angels nor demons, neither the present nor the future, nor any powers, neither height nor depth, nor anything else in all creation, will be able to separate us from the love of God that is in Christ Jesus our Lord."

(Romans 8:38-39)

"But you are a chosen people, a royal priesthood, a holy nation, God's special possession, that you may declare the praises of Him who called you out of darkness into His wonderful light."

(1 Peter 2:9)

I am honored to say today with a newfound boldness that **I AM BATTLE-SCAR FREE!**

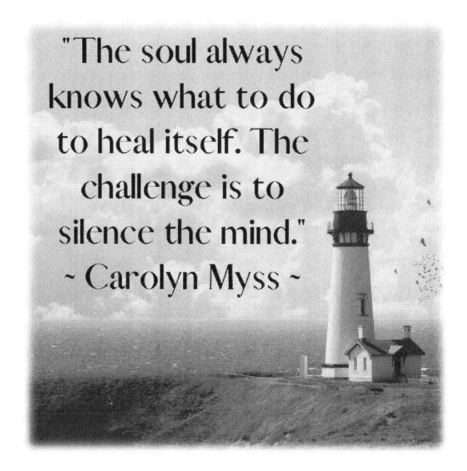

Tanya Holland
The Narcissist

"It's time to reclaim our Soul, and our Humanity."
~ **Michael DeMolina, Psychologist** ~
http://awisdomcenter.com/michael-demolina/

What is it like to be in a relationship with a **pathological narcissist**? Well, let me tell you…

- You will never win.
- You will never be loyal enough.
- You will never come to agreement enough times.
- You will never accommodate them enough to make them happy.
- You can't give them enough, pay them enough, or sacrifice enough.
- No matter how many times you fold in on yourself and lose your sense of identity — the very sense of who you are at your core — it will never be enough.

The pathological narcissist will never be appeased until everything around them is burned to the ground. They will leave you hungry, starving, empty, hollow, and guilty for not figuring out that "one more thing" you could have given. Even then, you will be asked for more and more…*and more.*

Far too many people have been saying those things for years. It's not a political issue; it's a **MENTAL ILLNESS**. Also, this **IS** my lane.

Webster's Dictionary defines a narcissist as: *"An extremely self-centered person who has an exaggerated sense of self-importance."*

The purpose of telling my story is not to school everyone on what a narcissist is. I am, however, going to share how I survived and was eventually able to leave my mentally, spiritually, and sometimes physically abusive marriage to one. At first glance, most people would have never thought (including me) that a disabled, wheelchair-bound pastor would be able to break someone to the point of near-suicide. I am thankful to our Lord and Savior that I am here to give my testimony.

And so, my story begins…

For the sake of storytelling, I will name my handsome, charming abuser "Marshall." Our relationship dates back to my high school years. He was a year ahead of me and went to a different school. He was a popular wrestler and also a friend of my older brother. We dated on and off until he graduated and enlisted in the U.S. Navy.

Fast-forward 30 years…

Marshall's reappearance in my life came when I was starting to wonder and ask God about my life's purpose. My son was grown and living on his own, I was unmarried, and I just felt like there was more for me to do than work a "9-5" job.

One day, out of the blue, I received a message on Facebook from my long-lost high school heartthrob. From there, Marshall and I chatted back and forth on Facebook for a while. Eventually, we exchanged numbers and began conversing on the phone. As I listened to his life's story, my heart just *broke*. He also asked me **ALL** the right questions, learned **ALL** about my story, and said and did **ALL** the right things in response. Almost effortlessly, Marshall wooed and reeled me in as if he were a lost puppy with a hurt paw.

A significant aspect of his past was the accident he suffered while enlisted that left him permanently disabled. Being the empathetic woman I am, I felt sorry for him and his situation. He went on to explain how he lost everything except his church building and a few of his loyal members. As a result of his "situation," his family fell apart, including the passing of his ex-wife who died in a tragic car accident. Marshall suffered so much tragedy…and there I was, looking to be someone's hero—and he **KNEW** it. He *KNEW* my vulnerability because I had openly and honestly shared it with him.

Marshall played on all my weaknesses, and four months later, we were walking/rolling down the aisle to exchange marital vows. It all happened so quickly and easily, I thought to myself, *"This **HAS** to be God's plan!"*

As I look back now, I remember seeing the red warning flags flapping wildly in my view, but I was so wrapped up in my "new purpose" and full of oxytocin (the chemical our brain releases when first falling in "love" with someone), those red flags appeared as white as snow—or maybe it was just him **telling** me they were. That was where his manipulative ways started.

I recall the first time he lied to and manipulated me. Marshall had a home health aide who had been with him for four years before we got married. During that time, they had developed a friendship and a "bond." As the aide was leaving one evening, Marshall went outside with her, saying she needed to give him something. After almost an hour went by, I started to wonder what was going on, so I walked outside. I didn't see either of them initially, but when I looked down the street, there they were…smoking weed. I went back inside and awaited his reemergence into our home.

It must be noted here that he had mentioned going to see a pain specialist to see about getting medical marijuana for his chronic discomfort, so I knew he wanted to use it for **THAT**. Not once did I consider recreational use with his *AIDE!*

When Marshall came back inside, I asked him **three times** about him smoking weed with her. Each time, he flat out **LIED** and made it seem as if I were seeing things.

"You saw my breath in the cold night air," he explained. *"She was smoking, so you probably saw her smoke near me."*

I must admit: That was the first time he made me feel like I was the crazy one.

Over time, the manipulation and mind games became an everyday occurrence. Not a day went by when we didn't have an argument that began with something **HE** did and end with **ME** being the reason why "everything" was wrong. For example, if I didn't get enough sleep and was tired the next morning, it was because I didn't listen to him when he told me to go to bed—even though my daily routine included tasks such as:

- Working a full-time job.
- Making dinner and setting his place at the table.
- Making sure his son (who had special needs) ate his dinner, showered, and took his medication.
- Cleaning up afterward.
- Tending to my husband's wound care.
- Turning and positioning him in bed and making sure he had his medication, water at his bedside, and remote controls.

After all of that, I still had to prepare myself for the next day and for bed, but that was hard to do when every five minutes, Marshall would call out to me because he dropped a remote, toppled a pill bottle, or spilled his water. I can't forget the times he simply wanted to find out what I was doing when out of his eyesight. When I would get frustrated, he found a way to play the victim, and yet another argument would begin. All I wanted was a *few* minutes to myself and then go to bed, but two hours later, I was left with much less than a full night's sleep in preparation for a new day. That "routine" went on for more than four years, and I grew exhausted.

Then came the "never enough" part. Every birthday was never good enough. No matter what I did or didn't do, it was never good enough. I remember how, on his 50th birthday, he volunteered to do the prayer at a wedding, so I made reservations for dinner and a movie after the event. Well, let me tell you this: He made sure I knew he was miserable, all because there wasn't a big party waiting for him at the restaurant. I have no idea how he expected me to pull that off while working and taking care of him, the house, the church, and the bills! That's not to mention when I asked him if he would like to do something special for his birthday, he said, *"Let's just go to dinner after the wedding. You already have enough to do."* Yes, it was **HIS** idea. No, it wasn't good enough.

He often complained about everything under the sun. Everywhere we went to eat, whether it was a fast food or fancy restaurant, he made a complaint or changed the food choice on the menu to what he wanted specifically. At times, it was so *embarrassing*. Then, if he didn't get his way, he would ask to speak to the manager or sometimes leave without even eating. After a while, I stopped wanting to go out to eat and, of course, was seen as being unreasonable and neglectful. So, what did he do? He started taking his home health aide to dinner instead!

Remember I said you could never sacrifice enough for a narcissist? *Well…*

Marshall often got infections because of a catheter or wound, so when he would have to go to the hospital, I would go with him initially to ensure they had all his medications correct and get him settled in his room. The first time that happened, everything was fine — until he called me at 2:30 a.m. saying no one had been to his room for four hours. I then called the nurses' station and was told his nurse just left his room after giving him his scheduled dose of pain medication. When I called him back, he quickly said they were lying. I had to go to work in the morning and told him I was too tired to come to the hospital at that time. He slammed the phone down in my ear.

An hour later, he called back and said, *"I keep turning on the call light, but they keep turning it right back off at the desk."* So, I call the nurses' station **again**. I was told they can't turn off the light from the desk and that they *have* to go into the room to do so (being a nurse, I already knew that). By the time I called him back, he said someone was in his room and apologized for waking me up. That night, I got a measly 3 ½ hours' worth of sleep before going to work.

Later that morning, he called me while I was on the job and asked if I would come to the hospital when I got off because they were not taking care of him. So, I went to find out what was happening, and he's there throwing a fit, yelling at the staff, and accusing people of not doing their jobs. When he saw me, he then pulled me into his madness. I spoke to the supervisor, and she filled me in. Basically, he wanted to get out of bed and into his wheelchair, but they didn't have the trained staff to do that. I told them I could do it and was told it would be a liability if I did (something I already knew but wanted him to hear it for himself). That didn't matter to him, though. He wanted out of that bed. I couldn't believe he acted that way!

Marshall was eventually told he could go home if someone was available to do the IV antibiotics. Well, of course he said, *"My wife is a nurse. She can do it."* That was the first of many times he was sent home with **more** care for me to do, all because of his outlandish behavior in the hospital — and because he refused to go to a nursing facility for a few weeks to finish the antibiotics or continue his wound care. I was already exhausted, but that didn't matter. I could never sacrifice enough for him.

Physically, the demands of life began to take their toll on me. My hair started falling out. My eyebrows were gone. I started having stomach issues that sent me to the emergency room. I already suffered from migraines, which were now on a level *beyond* ten. He then instructs me to ask his home health aide for help. The woman wouldn't even show up on time, but he still helped her get her car fixed and gave her money to get her daughter's hair done. He even took her to dinner and the movies, but whenever I asked her to do something, I was met with an eye roll and an attitude.

Then, there were his anger issues. When I wouldn't agree to or go along with his "plan" to do something (which usually consisted of cheating someone or trying to get out of doing something), he would become enraged. He would flip over tables, throw things at me, tell me I wasn't honoring him as a husband, and so on. That mistreatment would go on for days sometimes. He even had the audacity to have his home health aide try to "talk" to me. I knew the two of them had always been close, but I started to realize their closeness was getting much too cozy.

I later learned they would talk for hours on the phone, in addition to going to the dinner and the movies. He explained it away. *"Sometimes, she needs to talk about her family situation and kids."* One day, I overheard one of their conversations they were having in our home. They were talking about **ME**! Marshall told her how I sometimes came home late from work, to which she replied, *"Oh? She must be out there running around on you!"* **What nonsense!** So, when I walked in on that conversation and explained how tired I was and that sometimes, it was hard for me to keep up with the pace at work, they both "suggested" I get more rest. **REALLY? YOU THINK?** I couldn't believe my ears! Could anyone else see what was going on? Did no one see **ALL** that I was doing and understand why I was outright **EXHAUSTED?!**

The Transition

One day, after getting Marshall dressed and into his wheelchair (and, of course, after an argument), he tells me, *"I'm tired of this toxic relationship. I can't take it anymore."* I was already at my breaking point when he said that and responded angrily, **"Don't worry. I'll take care of that for you right now!"** I grabbed my gun, loaded it, and stuck it in my mouth. With swiftness, he came over to me and pulled my arm down.

That's when I knew it was time to leave. The relationship had reached its end.

The next day, I called my employee help number and connected with a mental health counselor. I then started making plans on how I was going to leave. I wasn't nervous, scared, or desperate because I knew my very life depended on me leaving sooner — not later. The sooner, the better.

What I'm about to say may sound uncaring and harsh.

My "out" came when Marshall had to go back into the hospital. I knew when he was released, there would be even more for me to do, and I just couldn't endure more sleepless nights. So, when he left for the hospital, I **immediately** began packing my bags. I then called my son and best friend to let them know my plans. The day Marshall was supposed to return home, I left…*and never looked back.*

Present Day

It's been over a year, and I'm still healing from Marshall's mind manipulation and mental abuse. For a moment, I actually started to feel bad and guilty about writing this testimony. At times, I thought, *"This doesn't sound **that** bad. Maybe he wasn't such an awful person."*

When I stopped my irrational thinking and reminded myself that he no longer has control over my thoughts and that what he did to me was real and traumatizing—and could have landed me in a grave—I now know I am, indeed, **Battle-Scar Free** and ready for whatever God **truly** has in store for my future and me.

Reyna Harris-Goynes
Free from Toxicity

For as long as I can remember, I tried so hard to make my mom change her ways toward me. The **transformation** within me came when I realized she would only change when she was **ready**, not because I *wanted* her to do so.

There was a time when I used to think I was always in the wrong while growing up because my mom treated me differently than she did my sisters. I vividly recall going different places and my sisters getting better treatment or more "stuff" than I did—and that is when it hit me: **That wasn't right!**

When my sisters and I went school shopping with our mom, there were times I did not get anything because my mom outright told me she was only buying for my sisters. I am grateful for my aunt's intervention. It was she who would say, *"Come ride with us* [her and her daughter/my cousin] *to go shopping."* That was how I was able to get clothes for school. One particular year, my mom bought me **one** thing for school, only because I *needed* them: shoes. I used to wonder, *"If I didn't* **NEED** *them, would she have bought them for me?"*

As mothers often do, my mom used to try and tell me who I could and could not be friends with. When my boyfriends started coming around, she really hated that. She had an utter dislike for some of my guy friends because they lived that "street life." It seemed my mom had a problem with **EVERYBODY** I chose to hang out with and told me, *"You need to pick better friends."*

The relationship between my mom and I became toxic because I grew tired of her always having something negative to say to or about me. At the age of 18, I had my first child. Oh, my goodness! What did I do **THAT** for? The negativity only got worse. When I turned 19 years old, I moved out of my mom's house and into my grandma's until I could get my own place. Oddly enough, my mom did not agree with my decision to move. For a little while, I also lived with my child's father and his mother, but that did not last long because of his controlling ways. Eventually, I did get my own place, yet the relationship remained severed between my mom and me.

I recall when I started dating my oldest son's father, it was not long before our relationship spiraled out of control. As stated, he was very controlling. My mom knew that about him — and even tried to warn me — but I did not listen, mainly because I just **KNEW** her opinion of him was *all* wrong. Well, it turned out she was **right**. That accurate assessment came when he started putting his hands on me when things did not "go his way." Yes, I became a victim of domestic violence and abuse. In March 1997, my son's father was in a horrific car accident that left him paralyzed from the neck down. Although paralyzed, he still found a way to control me and seemingly **ALWAYS** had a problem with everything I did. I think I remained with him for about a year after the accident. Before I finally walked away, he asked me to marry him. At the time, my immediate answer was yes…but that quickly turned to a **no**. My decision was final. I was done.

When I started talking to someone else, the relationship between my mom and me got even worse. Much like the other guys in my life, I knew she did not like him, but unlike the others, she never told me *why*. After giving birth to a baby girl by him, that relationship spiraled out of control, too. There were times my mom used to tell my children that I was **stupid** and **dumb** for staying with him, which soon led to my mom and I not communicating whatsoever for a whole year. During that moment of "silence," I gave birth to another child by the same guy.

Sadly, my oldest son suffered from neglect on both sides of the family. It seemed as if they simply forgot he existed. Some members of his father's side do not know him at all.

Fast forward to the present day…

My mom and I are communicating again, but our relationship will likely remain toxic to some degree because she is truly something else and stuck in her ways.

Today, I am married to my middle school sweetheart. Once again, my mom has a problem with our relationship. I do not know if it is because he was formerly incarcerated or what. Whatever it is, she will not express to me her "concerns" regarding him. Regardless of others' opinions of him, my husband is the love of my life. In stark contrast to those who came before him, he is totally different and shows me genuine love and affection. Did that change my mother's mind about how she feels about him? No. Nonetheless, I do not stop trying to tell her about his fine qualities, although she chooses not to listen.

Much to my disappointment all these years later, I have come to accept that my mother and I will not have the mother/daughter relationship I long for and truly desire.

Along this life's journey, I have learned that pleasing everyone else before indulging in self-care and doing the self-work will never amount to anything healthy. As it relates to my mom directly, I just go with the flow because my people-pleasing days are **over**. When she starts tripping out on me, I refuse to embrace those negative feelings toward me. I know for a fact that she and my sisters talk about me when I am not around, and although it used to hurt my feelings, I do not allow it to do so anymore. The older I get, the wiser I become in life. I know when I am not wanted around certain family members, especially at my mom's house *(and they wonder why I do not come around or show my face at different events)*. **Hmph...** My peace being disturbed is not worth the aggravation of being around those who do not want to be around me.

The lesson I have learned is this: I stay away from toxic people, even when that includes my own mother. I love her, though. She is, after all, the one and only mother I have. Still, now that I know better, I am doing better.

Battle-Scar Free means being *FREE* from *toxicity*, once and for all!

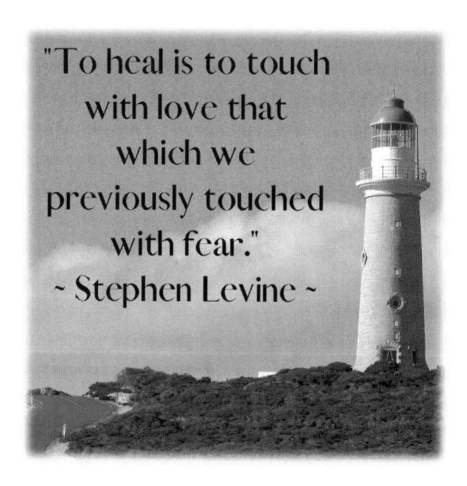

Alexandra Esperance
Selfish – A Poem

S.E.L.F.I.S.H.
Seven letters put together that I didn't know
Their depths 'til I met you.
S.E.L.F.I.S.H.
That's what you are.
Not a care in the world.
Not a worry about how your actions
Affect those around you.
Being careless with things
That don't belong to you.
Using and abusing me.
I should've known the first time you laid in my bed,
Wanting to satisfy you…and ONLY you.
Not knowing the meaning of 'intimacy,'
You pushed me aside after releasing your frustration.
You got up, got dressed, and told me you were done.
I asked, "What about me?"
You ignored me and said,
"You'll be alright."
Hopefully, you will find someone
Who shares the same values as you.
'Til then…
S.E.L.F.I.S.H.

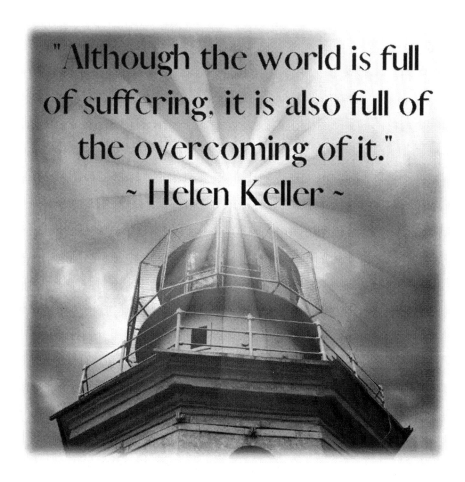

God Says I am Battle-Scar Free – Part Seven

Nikki Cheree
Breathing After Betrayal

Betrayal – A Poem

Sometimes, I think about where I would be

If the Lord had not captured and set my mind free

From the shackles of hatred, fear, and pain

That kept me in bondage and tethered to chains.

No one could tell me how to just move on,

When my life was shattered when I was so young.

Heartbroken by the betrayal of someone so close

Who chose to use manipulation and violate me the most.

I survived the assault with scars left behind,

And in impenetrable fear that consumed my mind.

Imagine a young girl whose life was changed forever,

When he came into my room and made us sleep together.

~ Nikki Cheree ~ © 2021

****

I can vividly recall the vilest instance of abuse that occurred in my life. I was nine years old, and the perpetrator (disguised as a favorite uncle) inappropriately touched me. What started as a touch—that made me feel weird—progressed to much more. When the fear and panic became evident, and the sexual violations grew more intense, my abuser resorted to threats against my mom, sister, and brother…not me. *"I will kill them if you tell anybody,"* he repeatedly boasted, all while assuring me it would be all my fault.

So, I never told. In fact, I lied when I was asked directly, *"Has anyone ever touched you inappropriately?"* All the while, my body was wracked with pain because of the assault….and the venereal disease left behind in its wake. The fear was so ingrained, it reached down into my soul. I vowed **NEVER** to tell and to protect my family.

That was until…

One day, my mother said to me with such tenderness and affection, *"No secret is greater than my love for you. You can tell me anything at all, and it will be okay."* After what felt like an eternity, I told it **all**. The terrifying spell was broken. The secret was out.

A court hearing ensued, where I was labeled "promiscuous" by an attorney in the courtroom. Then, nothing happened. My uncle was set free—free to abuse others again for many years to follow.

I was *DEVASTATED!*

After that day, I struggled to overcome shame, guilt, and fear for years. I worked with counselors, took self-help courses, and prayed to regain my sense of self-worth. An additional hardship came as my relationships suffered while I attempted to replace all the broken pieces of my life. Prayer allowed me to be open and honest with myself about myself. It was hard…real hard. I found myself starting over in life at least three times before finally embracing my new reality: I needed to turn my life around for the better, with no regrets.

The present-day pandemic (COVID-19/Coronavirus) took me back to the basics as I prepared this reflection. My goal is to share with you honestly and allow you to see that time truly does heal. If you want to continue to stay focused on moving forward, you will get there. Do not give up! I am standing with you! Please hear my heart through my words as I share with you my reflections of the past, present, and future. I pray you will be aided in becoming **BATTLE-SCAR FREE**…just like me.

The Past: *Memories*

The memories of what I endured as a child and young adult never eluded the recesses of my mind. I did, however, suppress them and walked around "numb." The stings of rejection and self-doubt followed me around like a shadow that trailed me in darkness rather than light. Although it had been years since my physical abuse, the remnants perpetuated in my self-confidence and relationships over time. It felt like I was forced into a state of recovery for the rest of my life.

No one *really* understood how the stain of abuse managed to leave a permanent mark on my life. Yes, I am a survivor, an overcomer, and more, **BUT** I am also always conscious of the fact that I never want to repeat that time in my life again. After all, it has lived in the recesses of my mind ever since I was a child.

I specifically asked God to give me the strength to walk out the manifestation of His healing and deliverance every day. I believed I was delivered from bondage but did not take for granted just how fragile my sense of self-worth really was. As I moved from level to level, fear crept back up. When my marriage hit a hard spot, the thoughts of rejection overwhelmed me. It was only when I retreated to my secret place that restoration finally occurred.

You see, I realized I had to be refreshed and restored. The woman I became was on the frontlines, helping other people to overcome their burdens of pain. **P**eople, **A**ttitudes, **I**nsecurities, and **N**egative perceptions will always be areas I must address head-on. That was the first time I really gave a name to the process as I navigated through the hardships of life. I began to sail through life as if nothing ever really happened. However, the abuse was a distant memory that seemingly jolted me back into reality instantly.

The residue of my recall was depression. I felt out of place or somehow in second place—like I never really had my "time to shine" and break out from being a victim. Many scars were left behind after I was abused so long ago, including domestic violence and three failed marriages. Still, I continued **LIVING** with the goal to help someone else survive. As I grew stronger, I was inspired to write a poem titled "When the Strong One is Broken." I wanted people to recognize the importance of checking on their strong friends because we never know what they are going through.

I will pivot to a place of power but must first truthfully share my past reality. Sometimes, I do remember…and it hurts. Sometimes, I realized I was overprotective when it came to my children, to the point of trying to control their every move.

Sometimes, I was fearful and had to pray my way through the flood of tears, well into adulthood. I wanted to be *FREE*. As a matter of fact, I **WAS** free because I chose freedom over death. If I had wallowed in what happened and the adverse effects, I would have never moved forward or accomplished my dreams.

When the release happened, God **TRULY** set me *FREE*.

The Present: *Challenges*

Today, I am realistic about life and know challenges will come—ones in vicious pursuit to steal my joy and consume all my time and energy, especially if the situation is outside of my control. So, I must think ahead, put contingency plans in place, and not leave my life in someone else's hands. God has shown me that there is a place to learn, grow, and stretch in every challenge.

For example, my financial problems did not matter to anyone who wanted a handout. I have since learned how to say "No!" and stopped trying to be a people-pleaser out of another's hardship. In my own life, hardships happen often, but they no longer change who I am or my quality of life. I am no longer that broken little girl waiting for her daddy to come to the rescue.

I have also come to understand what it means to overcome struggles out of sheer discomfort and lack. For every challenge, there is a solution. I just had to learn to be patient and plan. I turned my pain into passion and used every skill I have to create new environments. My place of strength came from every experience God allowed me to endure.

Decisions

To create a better lifestyle, my mindset had to change. That was when my chains were broken. My decisions reflected a new reality in my life. My previous abuse did not keep me stuck in childhood. I had to grow up and move past fear and pain. As I began to make better choices, my environment also changed for the better.

Coming from the space of an abused child and fragile young adult, I desperately wanted to make something out of my life. After a series of rocky relationships, I gave up the toxic ones with men who threw my past back in my face as a weapon of destruction. I finally turned the corner and found a mate who supported both my dreams and me. In essence, I began to breathe again. **Whew!** Being able to breathe helps me get through.

"Breathe, daughter." That is what I hear God saying to me.

I look back at everything I had to go through to get to something. Then, I take a deep breath…and smile. Yes, the Lord has kept me, and I did my work. I used vision boards as a method to see my way through to a better place. I also remind myself that death did not take me and that I have another opportunity to encourage and inspire others.

Blessings

"*The Lord is my Shepherd; I shall not want*" (Psalms 23:1).

Just like God's Word says, He never left me. I now walk in a place of peace versus brokenness. Even when the past comes to mind, I can see the grace that has been extended to me, and I no longer stay stuck when things do not go my way.

I no longer punish my mate for the wrongs done to me before he came into my life. I am free to love again…and be loved. Now, the security and confidence I seek come from within me first. My well is no longer dry. I did not seek my own justice, and now, my abuser is serving 50 years to life.

"*When the enemy comes in like a flood, the Spirit of the Lord will lift up a standard against him*" (Isaiah 59:19).

It is funny how people say, "*You cannot see what I have been through.*" Maybe you should try. As for me, I want to be an honest picture of reflection and evolution. I desire to show you:

- How you can make it through this tough time.
- How you can survive abuse and then thrive in life.
- How life throws us powerful blows, but we do not have to succumb to that force because God can pick us up when we get knocked down.

I am okay with you knowing my past pains. I have no fear of what may be written about me in blogs or on social media. Why? Because every misstep and mistake created a new path of opportunity for me to be exactly where I am supposed to be today. I do not wish abuse of any kind on anyone. I know all too well the hurt and pain it brings.

However, if you find yourself on the short end of that stick, please know:

- You can make it.
- You are worthy.
- You deserve joy and peace.
- You have hope inside of you.
- You are not alone.
- You have a powerful story to share.

Future: *Thrive*

My current vision board paints a beautiful picture of my life. Words alone cannot fully describe the bright future I see for myself. I am whole, complete, and full of hope. The generational curse of sexual abuse is broken off my family's seed. I see myself with a family of grown children as I enjoy my life as a grandmother. My marriage will endure the test of time, and our love will remain strong.

I also see myself financially-free with a thriving business after retiring from my corporate job. Most of all, I will be a woman walking in the purpose God placed inside of me. I will enjoy my journey and process. I profess I will never again suffer abuse at the hands of any man. My mission will be to share with those who come behind me how to move forward so that their struggle does not have to be as difficult as mine.

I have set those aspirations in motion by doing the work needed to progress and see my dreams come to fruition. My motto is, "You have to do something to move something." I implore you to examine where you are right now. Do not look to your left or right. Instead, sit upright, look straight ahead, and assess your current situation by asking yourself some simple questions like the ones that follow:

- What is holding me back?
- Where do I need to make a different choice?
- To whom have I given my power?
- What is one thing I can do differently today?
- When will I take my first step toward change?

Be Deliberate

It is your time to **DO SOMETHING** and create the future of your dreams. I envision you defining your goals, creating and planning, taking specific actions, and consistently moving one step forward every day. You are a *CONQUEROR* who is on your way to living **BATTLE-SCAR FREE!**

In Closing…

I am grateful for the opportunity to reflect on my experiences. For years, there have been both struggles and triumphs. There have also been invaluable lessons and principles I have followed along the way. My story, however, is simple:

I was abused, and I survived.

There were no magic pills or mystic steps that helped me change from surviving to thriving. It took years, consistency, and a will to live (not just exist). For me, God's grace and favor were the keys to my **FREEDOM**.

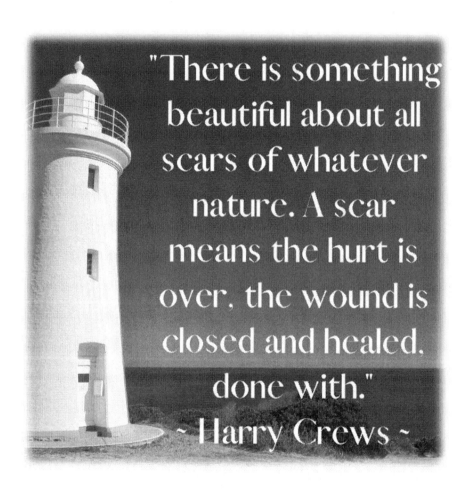

God Says I am Battle-Scar Free – Part Seven

Marlowe Scott
The Abusive Tongue: Words Matter

"Likewise, the tongue is a small part of the body, but it makes great boasts. Consider what a great forest is set on fire by a small spark."
(James 3:5)

Introduction

At the time of this writing, America and the world are experiencing many upheavals spewed by hatred. Countless repulsive words are being vocalized at rallies, demonstrations, and even through the various media outlets. Most recently in the U.S.A., an out-of-control mob of demonstrators went to the Capitol building in Washington, D.C., egged on by *words* spoken by a twice-impeached, one-term United States President!

Another ongoing cry has been heard from those fighting racism and other inequalities involving African Americans who were instrumental in building the U.S.A. into the great nation it is today. Sadly, those same people have not been considered "equal" or deserving of their labors and services for years. Their resounding cry is *"Black Lives Matter!"*

Just from those two illustrations, there are instances of lives lost because of **WORDS**!

Three of my personal experiences are shared in this story. Perhaps you will be able to remember similar instances in your life or the life of someone you know. You are encouraged to use the action pages included at the end of this story to reflect on those times.

As part of this 7th and final edition of the *God Says I Am Battle-Scar Free* series, there is a poem entitled **"Abuse Is Not Love."** It is special to me, as God inspired me to write it on my 71st birthday in 2015. The poem has been adopted as the centralized theme for the series and appears in **every** edition since being written. (It is included earlier in this book as well.)

Abuse Defined

The word "abuse" has many definitions. Its many forms are endless, including physical, mental, emotional, and (in modern times) cyber-bullying—to the point some have committed suicide. A partial list of the meaning of abuse includes:

- Treating others badly
- Saying and even writing hurtful words
- Degrading in public
- Legal injustices
- Victimizing young children
- Physically hitting, breaking bones, bruising, etc.

We know the tongue is small and has uses besides helping us to speak. History has shown how, during slavery, the tongue was sometimes cut in the mouths of slaves as punishment! While growing up in the country setting, I heard sayings, such as, *"Loose lips sink ships."* That expression was meant to remind us to be careful about talking too much.

The Holy Scriptures have many mentions referencing the tongue. One is found in Ephesians 6:4 concerning a warning to parents:

"Fathers, do not exasperate your children. Instead, bring them up in the training and instruction of the Lord."

As some of the stories in this 7th Edition share, there are fathers (and others) rearing children who do not adhere to that verse's teachings.

Yet another comes from Colossians 3:21:

"Fathers, do not embitter your children, or they will become discouraged."

The improper use of words can embitter children **and** adults. Although scriptures use fathers as the ones being addressed, the same applies to mothers, friends, employers, and interactions with others, including strangers.

Following are a few other passages of scripture about the tongue for your reference (it is wise to have a good Reference Bible and Concordance of your own to find others):

"Sin is not ended by multiplying words, but the prudent hold their tongues." (Proverbs 10:19)

"The words of the reckless pierce like swords, but the tongue of the wise brings healing." (Proverbs 12:18)

"For your hands are stained with blood, your fingers with guilt. Your lips have spoken falsely, and your tongue mutters wicked things." (Isaiah 59:3)

"Those who consider themselves religious and yet do not keep a tight rein on their tongue deceive themselves, and their religion is worthless." (James 1:26)

Personal Ways WORDS Were Abusive Toward Me

1. As a child from a small town of mostly Caucasian families, my friends from school were largely of that persuasion. At the time, the girls were involved in Brownies (younger Girl Scouts), and I persuaded my mother to let me go to a meeting with them one day. I was the only Negro in attendance. During the activities, one of the girls called another the "N-word." Everyone looked shocked, but I said nothing. Note that only one

word was spoken, yet it was perceived as negative and "less than," even at the tender age of eight. Upon returning home, I told my mother I did not want to go to any more meetings. When she asked me why, I dodged the whole truth and simply told her, *"I did not like it there."*

2. Later, as a chubby, overweight girl, I attended junior high and high school with atypical smart-mouthed peers. There was a song out at the time titled "16 Tons," and some of the boys started calling me that! Thankfully, my mother and other family members instilled in me self-respect and the family motto: *"No one is better than you, and you are no better than anyone else."* In time, I learned to smile at their teasing and I kept on moving. Gradually, only a few continued to taunt me after discovering I was not bothered by the name-calling. I must share here that by the time 12th-grade graduation came, I was 140 pounds with a 25-inch waist. Some of those same boys who teased me looked at me differently then—**and I ignored them!**

3. This last example really hurt the most because it involved my love of God and serving in the church—specifically the choir. The church I attended at the time had a choir director who required we practice before

singing on Sunday. With my job, family responsibilities, and not living close to the church, I missed many rehearsals.

One Sunday, I went downstairs to help with Sunday School. Some of the choir members were upstairs practicing familiar hymns for the service. After Sunday School, Miss Pauline — a sweet, gentle superintendent — encouraged me to sing with the choir that day. I reminded her of the rule, but she said it would be okay because she put on her robe and went to the choir box late every Sunday after tidying up after classes were over. Plus, she further assured me it would be alright because I was walking in with *her*.

So, as I passed the choir director, ready to step up into the choir box, she called me aside and told me I could not sing because I had missed practice. I explained to her that I was downstairs but heard the hymns and knew them all — and that Miss Pauline said it was alright to come up. Her rude response? *"Miss Pauline is not the choir director."*

My spirit was **crushed**. I turned around and walked down the center aisle with tears beginning to fall as the pastor, choir, church members, and ushers stared at me. Once outside the sanctuary, I sat down and let the tears fall freely. I recall an usher coming out and giving me some tissues.

After I gathered myself together, I asked the ushers at the door to bring me my children. I left the church that day with a hurt inside that felt like a knife had stabbed me in my heart!

Over the next few weeks following that incident, the pastor, officers, and other members called and tried to encourage me to return, but I refused.

After a few months, I found another church in my town to worship in and was again spiritually nourished and actively served God. I was an usher, choir member (eventually gaining the title of President), Sunday School Teacher, Missionary, and a District Lay President. I also attended many state and national conferences as a delegate.

BUT this story does not end there…

That same choir director was a friend of a newly-appointed pastor at the church I joined in my town, and she became the organist there! To not prolong the story, I will share with you a true saying my mother had:

"Don't be a church-jumper."

That simply means there are people and problems in **all** churches—something I have discovered to be accurate after communicating with family and friends over the years.

Needless to say, I was blessed by God despite what happened between the choir director and me.

Satan: The Musical Angel

Because my third experience involved **words** spoken to me and music, the following information is presented to those who may not know that Satan was a musical being in Heaven before being cast down. He was beautiful, with gems and musical instruments all around him. Satan was cast out of Heaven with other spiritual beings because he thought himself to be above God!

A sidenote from personal knowledge: I know of churches that have split because of problems that began with the choir. That pleases Satan, as he and his imps cause issues in churches.

Satan is a spirit at work in the hearts of those who refuse to obey God. The New Testament Book of Ephesians 2:2 states:

"...in which you used to live when you followed the ways of this world and of the ruler of the kingdom of the air, the spirit who is now at work in those who are disobedient."

The portion of that passage that grabs my attention is the words *"the ruler of the kingdom of the air."* Consider the cyber crimes and the newest virus that is spread through the **air** worldwide: **COVID-19.** That dreadful disease has taken countless lives — from children to the elderly — and the numbers continue to rise daily. Many are still dying, even as new vaccines are being tested and approved for distribution.

Taking Action

As mentioned earlier, the following are ways for you to consider how you can address abusive situations. Take time to write your thoughts on the lines provided.

1. **How have you been abused by the tongue or any other way?**

   _____
   _____
   _____
   _____
   _____
   _____

2. What feelings did you have with the abuse that occurred?

___

3. In what ways did you seek to overcome the abuse?

___

Conclusion

Please be aware that abuse happens to children, too. It is not just an adult issue; it is an "all people issue," beginning at infancy for some.

You are encouraged to attend Bible Studies and Christ-centered churches. If you are uncomfortable in a particular church, seek another. I did and was **blessed**! Should you not choose to do so at this time, develop a set devotional time for prayer and reading scriptures and devotionals. They can be found on the internet, booklets offered by some preachers on television, and you can sign up for daily emails to start your day. *(I have sometimes found inspiration for some of my ten published books by reading my devotional messages.)*

I pray my words have made a difference in your life and that you continue to grow as a person, love God, know Jesus as your personal Lord and Savior, and experience the Holy Spirit's presence in your life. I close with a partial quote from Proverbs 15:4, as I find it encouraging and something great to think about:

"A gentle tongue is a tree of life, but perverseness in it breaks the spirit…"

"Give it air and let the scar on your soul reveal itself because, like the body, it was made to heal itself."
~ Curtis Tyrone Jones ~

Laura Moseley
My Story of Pain and Promise

It's not uncommon for those with domestic violence survivor stories to say, *"Were it not for the grace of God, I would not be alive today,"* **BUT** in my case, that is the truest, most accurate statement of my survival! I credit Him for all my successes, even as I learned from my failures. It was God who kept my children and me safe from serious harm.

My story could have ended sooner—had I not been so stubborn in my refusal to listen more attentively to the Lord.

****

My childhood was one filled with love. I have parents who are still married and healthy, so I am blessed with that, too. From them, I was shown an example of what a loving relationship should look like and how, despite disagreements and differences, they never gave up on one another. They are each other's best friend and confidant as well. I just knew I wanted what they have and would have it for my own one day!

When I was 16 years old, I had a **horrific** encounter that I believe set a precedent for my abuse survivor story (or at least catapulted it):

I was raped by a boy I had gone on dates with and who I wanted to be my steady boyfriend.

To this day, those words are *STILL* hard to say, much less write.

When I told him, *"I am not ready to have sex,"* he decided to take what he wanted. It was a horrible experience that caused me to not date nor trust males (in general) during my high school years.

February of my senior year in high school, I met my abuser on our job at a plant nursery. I was a cashier, and he was tasked with caring for and selling landscaping plants. He lived with his newly-divorced brother and another roommate, providing support and splitting the rent. He seemed shy, sweet, and gentlemanly around me but was outgoing otherwise, so I gave him a chance when he finally found the courage to ask me out on a date. Instantly, my parents were not at all impressed with him. I just thought they were being overly-protective!

Before meeting him, I dated another guy who worked there, but that young man broke it off with me to be with another girl. After that happened, I decided I would go to my senior prom alone and not date anyone else…that was until I met my abuser.

He and I got serious quickly, and he was the first one I finally allowed to touch me sexually after my rape. He was gentle and sweet and promised *never* to hurt me. Within a few months, we found out I was pregnant. He had already proposed to me one month into our dating relationship (which should have been a sign of impending danger all in itself), but I found myself feeling **obligated** to accept since we had a baby on the way. I did not want our child growing up without a father or me gaining a reputation of being a "whore" — something I already thought about myself due to being raped. I believed I knew that man well enough to marry, so we exchanged vows in February of the following year, a few months before our first child was born.

Throughout our courtship and my pregnancy, he was wonderfully sweet and patient. Even after we had our baby and were evicted from our apartment, he did his best to obtain and keep jobs. Eventually, we moved in with his mother in Indiana. I really did not want to live with her, as I was embarrassed about our "situation," but it seemed necessary and, hopefully, temporary. While there, I restarted college, as my pregnancy previously interrupted my higher education venture. Plus, I thought that while living with her, we could save money, and I could finally graduate.

As you can see, I was hopeful that everything would be okay and that our marriage would be like the one my parents have.

I could not have been more wrong…

My mother-in-law turned out to be controlling and very judgmental of me — so much so that she kicked me out of her house, locked the door, and kept my infant son inside. My abuser did not want to lose me, so he talked her into letting me back in. After that incident was when I noticed his demeanor toward me changed. In response, I started making plans to leave but somehow got sucked back into that changing household dynamic. My pride refused to allow me to take my baby back to my parents' home in defeat. That same pride stoked the love I had for my husband. Truth be told, I also secretly feared my child and I would not make it without him.

When our child was around 18 months old, physical abuse reared its ugly head. We argued about money quite a bit. I was going to school full-time and working three part-time college work studies while he worked full-time. His mother required more and more money from us to live with her. She said it was because of the household's growing expenses, but the truth leaned more toward supporting her casino habit. Plus, I think she thought I was not good enough for her son and that

I was young and naïve (which, admittedly, I was). I also believe she thought she could simply take my child and be rid of me by having her son divorce me and boot me out the door. *Hmph.* She had **NO** idea just how stubborn I could be! I was also required to clean the house, cook meals, and do the grocery shopping—none of which was ever good enough. I accomplished those tasks and more, all while caring for my baby and making the coveted Dean's List!

The first instance of physical abuse happened when his brother was visiting. On that occasion, they were going out to have a beer or two and drive around while getting high. I recall making a snide comment about "not wrecking the car." It was the only car we had, and he had control of it most of the time. Before leaving, he caught me while alone, grabbed my breast in a vice-like grip, and shoved me hard against the wall.

"Why don't you shut your smart mouth before it gets you into trouble!" he hissed.

His shove proved to quickly and forcefully knock the breath out of me completely. When I attempted to scream, talk, or even breathe regularly, it came out as a squeak. To compound my struggle, he grabbed my other breast, picked me up, and bashed me against the wall two more times. I did not realize how hard he was gripping me until he released me, dropped me to the floor, and left with his brother.

That same day, I went shopping with his brother's fiancée, but all I could do was cry and tell her about what happened. Thankfully, my son slept in his stroller while she and I had coffee and talked. When we returned home, she confronted him (she sweetly thought doing so would help me, but it only made things worse).

A few years later, we were able to move out on our own. I, of course, thought things would improve. Sadly, they did not. Remaining with him made me more mindful of what I said and did, such as being more purposeful with my job and cleaning the house. We argued less if our home was clean, the groceries were shopped, and meals were prepared. I didn't take issue with any of those things because I was brought up by a great example of a wife and mother. Still, things were never good enough for him.

I did not decorate our home well enough.

I had gained weight and was not pretty enough.

I did not keep myself up well enough (I enjoyed wearing t-shirts and jeans when I was not working).

What more could I do to prove myself "enough"?!

I made sure I made myself up constantly. I exercised. I planned "family game night." I took our child and did fun "mommy-child" activities with him, which turned out to be me spending too much time with our child and not enough with my husband. I planned fun, low-cost date nights with him a few times a month. Still, things were never enough.

We never seemed to have enough money, but he wanted to get out of our apartment and move into a house. I took on a part-time job, in addition to my full-time job, and ended up blindly giving him **ALL** the money. I operated on very little money, yet that was still not good enough. I worked until I nearly had a nervous breakdown, but we were finally able to purchase a tiny home!

That **HAD** to be the turning point in our lives…***RIGHT, LORD???***

Once in our own home, we were constantly behind on the bills. I did not realize he was buying marijuana with our money. I also did not know that when he was out on "boys' night," he was cheating on me by picking up women in bars and taking them to cheap hotels. How, then, was it that our joint checking account always in the red was **MY** fault? It was he who controlled the finances!

Another time I recall being physically assaulted was when he had beaten both my son and me for being gone too long and spending money. I called the police, kicked him out of the house, and had him taken to his mother's. By then, we had another child — our daughter.

His drug and alcohol habits had gotten so bad, he was fired from his job as a jail officer. He begged me to come back home and promised he would change. I wanted that! God, how I wanted to think that was true! I mistakenly allowed him to return, and he ended up getting addicted to prescription medicine for anger, which he mixed with alcohol. Due to our dire situation, he watched our infant daughter instead of paying for a sitter while I continued to work. What a horrible, desperate decision on my part!

One day, while working as a "help desk" professional, I received a call from my abuser. His speech was slurred, making understanding him nearly impossible. All I could make out was that our infant daughter would not stop crying. I rushed home to find her disoriented. I immediately took her to the pediatrician, whose form of "help" was the threat of calling Child Protective Services on me.

After confirming she was not hurt, I took her and my young son to his mother's house, where we stayed for a little over a month. By that time, my mother-in-law and I had come to an understanding that included a mutual love for my children. I also think she finally realized I was a much stronger person than she previously gave me credit for. Our departure came by way of my husband speaking negatively about me again, which prompted his mother to push us out of her home.

We returned to our home...*and back to his **empty promises** of changing.*

I noticed that while he worked harder and harder to get me to come back to him (and eventually, I would), the abuse grew progressively worse each time. All the while, he was slowly but surely destroying my self-esteem. I should have returned to my parents' home in Tennessee, but because I had gone back to my abuser time and time again, my pride would not allow it.

We ended up welcoming a third child (one he declared on many occasions was not his). I clearly recall the **torment** I endured during that pregnancy. He was less physically abusive while I was pregnant, but he loved to shove me down forcefully. I think he hoped I would lose the baby. Our third baby was delivered via c-section, so I was sent home with pain medication I believed I could easily regulate. I was in pain and suffered from depression, so I was pretty much dependent on him. During that time, he reverted to being his caring, sweet self and vowed to care for us.

You might not believe what happened next…

Between him and his brother, they took **ALL** of my pain medication! I had to recover from **MAJOR SURGERY** without pain meds! That was the most excruciating physical pain I have ever felt. ***EVER!***

As time progressed, the physical abuse got worse — thanks to drugs and alcohol. I had to constantly break up arguments between him and my children by physically getting in between them. Meanwhile, I worked multiple jobs to keep our bills paid because he began "working for himself" (after not maintaining a steady job with an employer due to either low attendance or his bad attitude). I had to work when he was not at home and be careful not to leave my children alone with him. I felt that if he were going to abuse anyone, I would rather have him focus his attention on me and not them.

Mental and verbal abuse were rampant during our marriage, as was financial. At one point, he was finally removed from our home for beating and choking me, and an emergency protective order was issued. I thought I was home free, but he ended up luring me back through his mother by stating he knew he had problems and had tried to end his own life.

He changed (or so I thought) because he had hit rock bottom. I was mistaken. Seemingly in the blink of an eye and without warning, allegations were plentiful that I was cheating on him. His response to those accusations was threatening to take the children away from me. The physical altercations we had were attributed to him *"trying to beat sense back into me."*

One argument, which started with him and our daughter arguing about her hiding what I was doing and her becoming a *"whore, just like your mother,"* placed me in between them once more. He struck me on the side of my head, and I lost hearing in that ear and had a loud ringing noise in it for weeks afterward. I thought I had a punctured eardrum, but that was not the case. However, my hearing is presently only 39% in my left ear and 78% in my right.

The end of the marriage almost ended in tragedy. The abuse, coupled with his incessant drinking, resulted in a level of chaos I never envisioned. The final altercation led to him shooting at me with a 9mm gun, him beating me in front of our youngest child, him destroying the house and trying to set it on fire, and the police having to chase him down after he ran. My life seemed so bleak and hopeless!

The Transition to Becoming Battle-Scar Free

Today, I am happy to report that after another protective order and having **NO** contact with my abuser, I was able to pull my life together. We are divorced, and my children and I are living our best lives without him (he lives in another state). I now have a job that includes helping others. There is **NO** violence in my home, only peace.

Say it with me:

God is good all the time, and all the time, God is good!

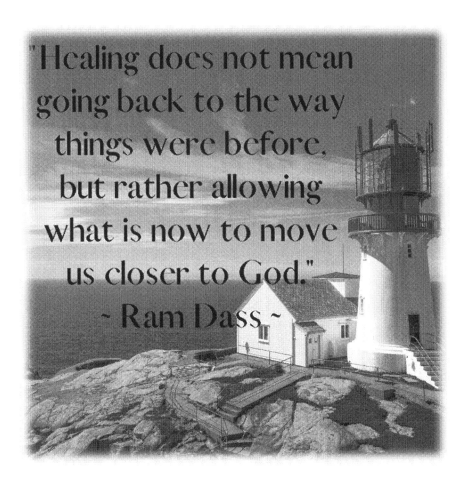

Angela R. Edwards

Alexandra Esperance
Betrayal – A Poem

Hurt.
Pain.
Betrayal.
Those words express the night that things went wrong…
The night you claim was 'my fault.'
How can someone who I once loved hurt me?
How can someone who promised my family he'd take care of me betray my trust?
With one stroke of your hand, you belittled me.
You made me believe I was nothing.
You ignored my cries.
You ignored my pleas.
You beat me.
You dragged me as though I were a rag doll.
Once you felt your job was accomplished,
You left me to die.
At first, I did not know there was someone greater than you.
It was God who gave me strength and courage and reminded me to be still.
He will fight my battles.
He reminded me that men like you don't deserve women like me —
A woman whose love is genuine…
Who would put your needs before hers.
Strong.
Brave.
Happy.
Those are the words that describe the way I felt
Once you were out of my life.

God Says I am Battle-Scar Free – Part Seven Conclusion

You, my Brother- or Sister-in-Christ, have reached the end of your new beginning! As one who holds multiple titles related to this work—Publisher, Compiler, and Contributor—it is my sincerest prayer that something penned on the pages of this book has resonated with your spirit and empowered you to keep the faith. Perhaps while reading, you received confirmation to make a change in your life…before it is too late. If so, I would love to hear from you! Send an email to BestSeller@PearlyGatesPublishing.com with **YOUR** overcomer testimony.

Again, I thank the **SURVIVORS** who shared their testimonies herein. This was as much a healing journey for them as it *IS* for the readers.

Abuse knows no boundary.

Abuse has no face.

Abuse knows no gender.

Abuse does **NOT** discriminate.

If you are being or have been emotionally, physically, mentally, or spiritually "injured" by another, **IT'S ABUSE.** In earnest, prayers are being laid at the feet of God for you, that

His angels will protect your heart, mind, soul, *AND* body as you prepare to make what **WE** hope is a life-changing, survivor-story decision.

For those who have shared their transparent truths with you here, revisiting those painful memories was not an easy process. *HOWEVER*, each found the strength to persevere with a threefold purpose:

1. To demonstrate to **YOU** that you are not alone.
2. To free **THEMSELVES** from the chains of silent bondage.
3. To allow the healing process to **TRULY** begin.

Dating back to this series' first release, each contributing author has worked diligently to effect change and **ERADICATE** abuse. That was proven evident by the countless messages, texts, phone calls, and emails received over the years that said, *"THANK YOU! BECAUSE OF MY STORY BEING TOLD, I'VE BEEN SET FREE!"* — confirmations that **GOD** did a marvelous work in their lives.

I applaud those who have never spoken of their personal abuse survivor stories until "now." It is not easy. I know because I was once in their shoes. As I reflect on this series, some initially agreed to be a part of the projects but, for whatever reason, had a change of mind and heart at the last minute. Perhaps they were not as "ready" as the projects required—which is okay! When they are prepared to shed those pains of the past once and for all, **GOD** will make a way out of no way for them to share.

In closing, we are blessed to be a blessing to others. Someone is waiting for your message of hope. Will you continue to deny them the opportunity to be **FREE**? I pray you come to acknowledge the power of **GOD** for yourself and one day *SOON* find the courage to tell your story. You can do it!

I am a **SURVIVOR**! The contributors to this project are **SURVIVORS!** *YOU* are a **SURVIVOR**, too! **NOW, TELL IT!**

God Bless, one and all!

God Says I am Battle-Scar Free – Part Seven

DEFINITION OF A SURVIVOR:

YOU!

My Plan to Break the Cycle of Abuse in My Life

1) _____
_____
_____

2) _____
_____
_____

3) _____
_____
_____

4) _____
_____
_____

5) _____
_____
_____

God Says I am Battle-Scar Free – Part Seven

6) _____

_____

_____

_____

7) _____

_____

_____

_____

8) _____

_____

_____

_____

9) _____

_____

_____

_____

10) _____

_____

_____

_____

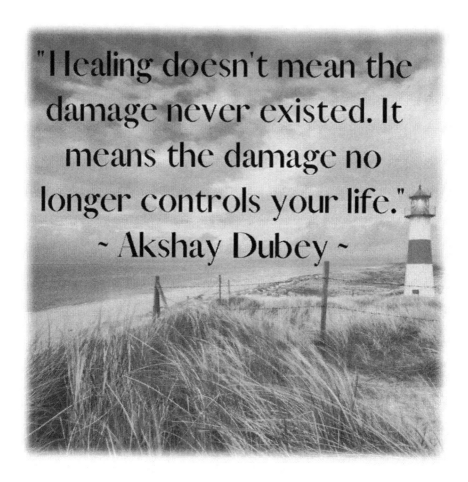

Following is a list *(in no particular order)* of National Domestic Abuse Resources. If and when the need arises, **PLEASE** take advantage of the opportunities presented here to be *FREE* from the abuse — or to help another in *NEED*. Silence is a device of the enemy. Use your voice. **BE FREE!**

National Domestic Abuse Resources

- **National Domestic Violence Hotline**
  Staffed 24 hours a day by trained counselors who can provide crisis assistance and information about shelters, legal advocacy, health care centers, and counseling.
  1-800-799-SAFE (7233)
  1-800-787-3224 (TDD)

- **Rape, Abuse & Incest National Network**
  The Rape, Abuse & Incest National Network (RAINN) is the nation's largest anti-sexual assault organization. Among its programs, RAINN created and operates the National Sexual Assault Hotline at 1-800-656-HOPE and the National Sexual Assault Online Hotline at rainn.org. This nationwide partnership of more than 1,100 local rape crisis centers provides victims of sexual assault with free, confidential services — 24 hours per day, 7 days per week. These hotlines have helped over 13 million people (and counting) since RAINN's founding in 1994.
  1-800-656-HOPE (4673)

- **National Coalition Against Domestic Violence**
  1120 Lincoln Street, Suite 1603
  Denver, CO 80203
  Phone: 303-839-1852
  TTY: 303-839-8459
  Fax: 303-831-9251
  Email: mainoffice@ncadv.org

- **1in6, Inc.**
  P.O. Box 222033
  Santa Clarita, CA 91322
  Support for male survivors of childhood sexual abuse and their families.
  24/7 Online Support
  www.1in6.org

- **National Battered Women's Law Project**
  275 7th Avenue, Suite 1206
  New York, NY 10001
  Phone: 212-741-9480
  Fax: 212-741-6438

- **Safe Horizons**
  2 Lafayette Street, 3rd Floor
  New York, NY 10007
  Crime Victims Hotline: 1-800-621-4673
  Rape and Sexual Assault & Incest Hotline: 212-227-3000
  TTY (for all Hotlines): 1-866-604-5350
  Fax: 212-577-3897
  Email: help@safehorizons.org

- ❖ **National Resource Center on Domestic Violence**
  6400 Flank Drive, Suite 1300
  Harrisburg, PA 17112
  Phone: 1-800-537-2238
  Fax: 717-545-9456

- ❖ **Battered Women's Justice Project**
  c/o National Clearinghouse for the Defense of Battered Women
  125 South 9th Street, Suite 302
  Philadelphia, PA 19107
  Toll-Free: 1-800-903-0111 ext. 3
  Phone: 215-351-0010
  Fax: 215-351-0779
  National Clearinghouse is a national resource and advocacy center providing assistance to women defendants, their defense attorneys, and other members of their defense teams in an effort to ensure justice for battered women charged with crimes.

- ❖ **National Clearinghouse on Marital and Date Rape**
  2325 Oak Street
  Berkeley, CA 94708
  Phone: 510-524-1582

- ❖ **Faith Trust Institute**
  (Formerly Center for the Prevention of Sexual and Domestic Violence)
  2400 N. 45th Street #10
  Seattle, WA 98103
  Phone: 206-634-1903 ext. 10
  Fax: 206-634-0115
  Email: info@faithtrustinstitute.org

- ❖ **National Network to End Domestic Violence**
  1101 South Street NW, Suite 400
  Washington, DC 11009
  Phone: 202-543-5566
  Hotline: 1-800-799-SAFE (7233)
  TTY: 1-800-787-3224
  Fax: 202-543-5426

- ❖ **Womenspace National Network to End Violence Against Immigrant Women**
  1212 Stuyvesant Avenue
  Trenton, NJ 08618
  Phone: 609-394-0136
  24-Hour Mercer County Hotline: 609-394-9000
  Fax: 609-396-1093
  Email: info@womenspace.org

Connect with Pearly Gates Publishing

On the Web: www.PearlyGatesPublishing.com
Email: BestSeller@PearlyGatesPublishing.com
Facebook: @Pearly Gates Publishing
Instagram: @PGPublishing
Twitter: @PearlyPublish
Mail: P.O. Box 62287, Houston, TX 77205
Phone: 1-832-994-8797

The Faces of the Free

Following are the contributors *(in order of appearance)* who penned their stories in this project.

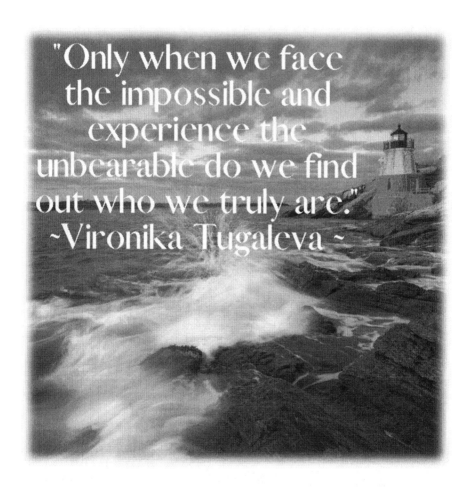

Made in the USA
Columbia, SC
25 May 2021